THE COST OF INDECISION

A PLAN FOR MUSIC & LIFE

TreNT

You ATE A BLESSING TO THE BODY.
THANK YOU FOT TAKING THE TIME
TO REVIEW MY BOOK. THANK
YOU FOT BEING AN EXAMPLE.

Michael Weatherspoon

Faith Walk
PUBLISHING

DEDICATION

I am honored to dedicate this book to my mother, Ethel Mae Weatherspoon, and my daughter Mackenzie Janai' Weatherspoon. Ethel Mae Weatherspoon, who at 18 years of age, became a licensed Christian Evangelist and has been dedicated to enriching the lives of people with a sincere heart ever since. Not looking for anything in return but to see the people blessed and their lives changed. At 22 years of age, you gave birth to me, but on the same day, your heart went into chaos, and a pacemaker was inserted to regulate it. You couldn't spend any time with your first born due to being in intensive care for four months. I spent so much time away from you that I thought your sister, Olivia, was my mother. And upon your release and I had to learn who you were, but that didn't take long. Through the years, your support, encouragement, prayer, and dedication have allowed some of what's in you...to now be in me.

Mackenzie Janai' Weatherspoon. I prayed for a daughter, and I received it. With only being on the Earth 10 years, you have literally kept me alive. Now I know what it means when the Elders would say, "Children are a blessing." Children have the ability to sustain Life. Even before you developed the ability to comprehend, in my darkest and troubled hours, it was your hugs, smiles and forgiving spirit that said, "Daddy, it's ok." With that said, I hope this book leaves a legacy for you. A seed you can sow into your children and your children's children for the betterment of those you and they encounter.

ENDORSEMENTS

"In this book, Michael has given the church/the world a gift - the gift of clarity and understanding surrounding a topic that most of us are uncomfortable with DECISION-MAKING. He is a trustworthy and respected teacher and music evangelist and is an intellectually gifted musician and producer, which gives him a unique platform and perspective worthy of our attention. This book promises to help your teams think through and act on a variety of issues that often paralyze and stagnate their progress...it will help create an environment for healing and resolution, helping them to move forward - "You have circled the mountain long enough" - Deuteronomy 2:3. It is destined to be a best-seller and will be one of the important books of this generation and should be read by pastors, directors/ministers of music, leaders and laity. I'm already looking forward to the sophomore project by this author!!"

Walter Owens, Jr.
Minister of Music and Arts
Salem Baptist Church of Chicago
Adjunct Faculty, Columbia College Chicago

"This book will challenge us all to be accountable to our life's purpose and stretch us to raise the bar to God's standard for our lives. Indecision has a generational effect on the lives of a people. To not make a decision, is a decision in itself. God has used Michael Weatherspoon, in this moment, in the history of the world, to give us fresh thought and relation that will affect lives for generations to come. Having known Michael for over ten years, he is a man that walks and speaks softly. But, when he is compelled to open his mouth, it awakens our desires that have been lulled to sleep by apathy.

Proverbs 13:12 tells us "Hope deferred makes the heart sick, but a dream fulfilled is a tree of life."

For those whose hope has been on layaway, this writing has made available THE TREE OF LIFE! Thanks, Mike!"

Jeffrey Newton,

Pastor of Ministries, Valley Kingdom Ministries International

"The mind and ministry of Author Michael Weatherspoon for me is astounding. His study and knowledge of the Word of God is in-depth and divided rightly. I am excited for every reader, leader, and ministry that will be empowered and elevated to new levels by the word given in this book through this man of God. Enjoy!"

Valencia Lacy

Worship Leader/Recording Artist

New Life Covenant Churches Southeast (Chicago)

"Michael and I previously served as leaders in a music ministry. One evening after a ministry meeting, Mike shared with me how

God was dealing with him regarding the Levites. He was studying the position, protocol and the importance of this role. Hearing his passion, he desired the members in music ministry to understand who they were truly called to be, using God's Word. I knew there was more that needed to be heard, and that's when Mike began teaching me portions of his study material. He created Music 101, and as a result of that course, this profound book will teach you how to hear from God, pray, fast, and reap the benefits of Mike's obedience to God. This book will provoke you to study the importance of God's purpose for your position as you answer the call to your assignment, reveal the importance of treating your anointing and the anointing of others with more respect, release God's expected lifestyle of a Levite and remind you that every plan from God is supported in the Bible.

"A man's gift makes room for him, bringing him before great men (Proverbs 18:16)"

Minister Kim R. English
Founder & CEO, My Steps Inc.

"This revelation from God, The Cost of Indecision: A Plan for Music & Life is a cutting-edge book for this season! It's absolutely rock solid for the Body of Christ! Michael Weatherspoon is right on target in this revealing manuscript! Every minstrel leader and fivefold leader should read this writing twice! Dealing with leaders and their unbalanced lives is one of the most important topics we could ever speak about. Michael deals with this subject masterfully! This is a great read! Looking for a change, you're holding it in your hands! Great work Minister Michael. God has used you to put the pieces together so leaders can function and fulfill their office with wisdom, revelation, knowledge and understanding!"

Christopher Hardy, International Covenant Life Network/ KAMT
Plano, Texas

"This teaching could not come at a better time! With all of the disorganization, division, confusion, and frankly, lack of understanding and respect for this divinely established ordinance, Michael Weatherspoon boldly and clearly re-aligns the kingdom of God with its original intent. It is impossible to receive this prolific teaching and remain the same. THIS IS A MUST READ FOR ALL MUSICIANS AND THOSE CALLED TO THE LEVITICAL PRIESTHOOD IN THE KINGDOM OF GOD!"

Pastor Christopher Montgomery
Kingdom Life Empowerment Fellowship International,
Goldsboro, NC.

"Often times in ministry and in music, we operate without ever taking the time to Count the Cost. Thank God for this timely work, inspired by God, to be a much-needed tool that many can glean from before truly entering a work that requires the absolute best from each of us. Michael is a gift to the body of Christ. Allow this reading to inspire you to truly 'count' the cost of ministry as well as understanding that God is a God of order which means God is a God of 'plans.' Read and Be Blessed."

Pastor Edwin Harris
St. Mark Baptist Church
Harvey, Illinois

"I am personally excited about a book being written from an unsuspected perspective about Order in music ministry. If the story is true about the "Little Drummer Boy" giving all he had to worship the King; the drummer's perspective has to be one that we need to hear. Michael Weatherspoon, we feel your heart when you play, and this book will allow us to read what we have felt."

Lamar Campbell
Gospel Recording Artist

"The root of indecision is not understanding your purpose and your path. Michael has picked up the torch of truth in helping to reveal God's purpose and intent for those with musical ability. He has a teacher's anointing and helps to bring clarity and focus to this "Mountain of Influence"."

Niles Bess
Prophet/Gospel Recording Artist

"Michael Weatherspoon is an innovative and skilled gospel music pundit who is filled with fresh material and information. Michael delivers enlightening facts creating definite cohesiveness from start to finish."

Dr. Dennis E. Cole

Stellar Awards Gospel Music Academy

President Emeritus-Chicago Gospel Announcers Guild of GMWA

"Michael Weatherspoon is a rare find. Rarely do you find someone who is immensely gifted and extremely integral. But I must say that Michael Weatherspoon is that man! He is an asset to the Body of Christ as well as the industry. Glad to know him and call him a friend."

Myron Butler

Grammy Award Winning Gospel Artist/Producer

"Michael has shown himself to be an example of operating in excellence and maintaining integrity in music ministry. I have witnessed his commitment to ministry, production, and heart to serve. If you take advantage of his years of experience and the knowledge he has to impart, I am certain it would be both impactful and beneficial to you and your ministry."

Tonya Baker

Gospel Recording Artist

Contents

FOREWORD

The Bible declares that Satan was covered in precious stones, and the workmanship of his tambourines and his pipes were prepared 'within' him when he was created (Ezekiel 28:13). Satan was not only heaven's minister of music, but he "was" music. We must understand that when Satan fell in rebellion against God, he did not lose the musical abilities that God had given him, but no longer used those abilities to glorify God; he used them to turn God's creatures against their Creator. It is with music that we glorify and worship God our creator. Therefore, our churches must be adequately equipped to lead God's people into worship through music.

I am so very excited about the vision that God has given Michael Weatherspoon to teach his people how to adequately bring God to the forefront through music. Having known Michael nearly 15 years, I have personally witnessed his passion for music, expertise to worship God with his musical talents, and his amazing gift to teach others how to enter into the presence of God through music. This book will teach pastors how to adequately position their musical staff to prepare the atmosphere for God to dwell in the midst of every service. Once you put into action the plans laid out by Michael, I believe the results will be life changing!

Pastor John F. Hannah,

Sr. Pastor, New Life Covenant Church Southeast

Producer. Musician. Educator. Clinician. Businessman. Father. Husband. Friend. All these and more bear the description of my longtime friend and brother Michael Weatherspoon. From his formative years until now, he has been a phenomenal percussionist, a source, and resource for many both in and outside the world of music.

Our history dates back nearly three decades to our start in the contemporary gospel group Michael Houston and Ministre, then on to a variety of musical collaborations throughout the years. Michael went on to work with the award-winning Shekinah Glory Ministry, under the leadership of Pastor Rose Harper. We were both a part of this dynamic entity for nearly two decades, along with his brother, renown keyboardist, and producer Daniel Weatherspoon. Spoonfed Productions went on to produce music for artists including, Shekinah Glory Ministry and my solo releases, Draw Nearer and Place of Worship.

Michael's musical resume spans the boundary of music in nearly every genre. He has produced and performed on an extensive number of projects both live and in the studio as well as stage plays covering the lives of historical figures such as "Fats" Waller and Billie Holiday.

In recent years, Michael has become a noted clinician, with

seminars in the area of worship instruction entitled Music 101, of which the material in this book entails. These presentations cover the role of the Levitical Priesthood and its application to the modern day worshipper. The consecration, dedication, meditation and practical application of the worshipper will be covered in this book.

This volume represents years of Michael's experience in all forms of study, and I believe you will find it a valued read. I salute my brother Michael on what I believe will be the first of many writings to come! Be inspired and enjoy!

Phil Tarver
Pastor, United Faith Ministries International
Recording Artist

ACKNOWLEDG-MENTS

As with most acknowledgments, you find a long list of people that are thanked who, most times, have never met the author or knew they even made an impact on them. I won't bore you with that. However, as with all acknowledgments, you thank the people that helped you get your book completed.

I thank God for allowing me to be a voice in this season and giving me the ability to speak things plain and clear so that people can receive it. I thank my parents for all of their support, but most of all for 45 years of marriage and being an example that you can make it if you choose to. I thank my one and only sibling Daniel, the greatest musician in the world, for being a great brother and having my back when I wasn't there to defend myself. I thank Mesha and our precious daughter Mackenzie. Both of you continued to push me to finish this book when I walked away from it so many times. Your assistance and encouragement were vital to the completion of this book. I'd like to thank Faith Walk Publishing for saying, "we have read your book, and we are interested." I want to thank Walter Owens for imparting, Jeff Newton for believing, Phil Tarver for blessing, Kim English for interceding and Demetrius Banks for listening. To every Pastor and music artist who allowed me to come and speak to your ministry, group or team...thank you. It helped me become refined so this book could be ready for dissemination to the world. But as most acknowledgments stop here, I won't.

Finally, I want to acknowledge the applied reader. Of course, I thank those that purchased the book and supported me regardless if they found the subject matter interesting. I thank those that will read the book for hobby or to simply increase their level of understanding of the subject matter. However, it is the reader who will administer and apply the standards and examples in this book to enhance their current environment that I want to offer praise to. Because it is YOU that will bring change, it is YOU that will bring success to fruition, it is YOU that will see those entities that YOU touch take definition and cause its purpose to take form and shape, for it is YOU that will cause indecision to become eradicated.

THE COST OF
INACTION

"Throughout history, it has been the inaction of those who could have acted; the indifference of those who should have known better; the silence of the voice of justice when it matter most; that has made it possible for evil to triumph"

Haile Selassie

Wᵉ can no longer say, "We didn't know." We can no longer protect our personal interests, paycheck, position, and influence. The Levitical assignment is far too great for us to stand by and do nothing, say nothing and be nothing in the presence of God.

We must remove ourselves from this perpetual cycle of emotional need fueled by the promise of prosperity that has permeated the Body of Christ around the country and the world. Bishop T.D. Jakes stated, "*The people in the Body of Christ are not mentally ill, but emotionally ill.*" And our hurt is misguided because it's not the devil that has caused this illness in most instances, for we give him far too much credit, but we are emotionally ill because we are suffering from the consequences of our decisions. And our disobedience has come to collect its ransom. So now we have to spoon feed the body with prosperity while we continue in the cycle of disobedience which produces results that we can't deal with in our daily lives. Our songs and our teachings are not about God's Word, but of inspiration and encouragement that, in turn, never brings us to a point of deliverance. God is not required to act when we are in disobedience. "Greater is coming" cannot be the NEW mantra when we have no conviction towards righteousness, holiness and order.

The Levitical priesthood has become unglued. We must use the Word of God as an adhesive to repair the cracks, the breach, and the punctures in the Temple and we must drag Satan out of the lair he has created in our pulpits, choir stands, music pits, treasuries and meeting rooms. We cannot allow Satan to gain any more momentum than he already has. He must be refuted at every gate, entry and access point, crack and crevasse, word and deed.

The cost of inaction so far has been great, priests have fallen, worship leaders command the glory, musicians and singers go the highest bidder, churches have closed, and pastors have walked away. Families have been broken; marriages have dissolved, and directors don't even know if they are a man or a woman. Intercessors have been overwhelmed at the temple gates due to lack of reinforcements, but what is continuing to happen? We're shouting, jumping and running. Our emotional response has increased while Order has decreased.

What is the cost of doing nothing? It breeds indecision and those that resist action are guaranteeing that Satan will play a bigger role. The young will have no future placement, families will become displaced, people will not be healed and delivered, ministries will not advance, and souls will be lost.

INTRODUCTION

During the summer of 2010, I was asked by Pastor Jeff Newton, Pastor of Ministries, at Valley Kingdom Ministries International (VKMI), to oversee the music department. Gospel Artist, Phil Tarver, who is now Pastor of United Faith Center Ministries International, was stepping down as Minister of Music at VKMI to begin focusing on his new assignment and needed a year to transition. During my time of preparation and before I was introduced to the public, God spoke to me and clearly stated that "People have been given positions in Levitical Priesthood... but do not know their assignments, nor have they been trained". So He began to have me write and when I was done, a 4-week class entitled, MUS 101 Introduction to Music Ministry, was completed.

In 2011, I began to teach this course to those newly admitted into the music ministry at VKMI, which consisted of Spirit & Truth (Youth/Young Adult Praise Team), Unity Choir, and Shekinah Glory Ministry. It resulted in the class being taught to the entire Unity Choir, and God blessed greatly. From there, various ministries around the Chicagoland area and gospel artists began to contact me to speak on this topic to help edify their members. In

2012, God spoke again about the teaching being converted into a book and here we are.

The aim of this book is to provide an overview of the origins of the music ministry while providing a historical perspective with practical applications on Levitical priesthood and how it relates to the modern day Christian Church. This book is to serve as an orientation to new and current music ministry members on the range and scope of their individual Levitical assignment and responsibilities as it relates to a specific ministry. But more importantly, this book is to help leadership understand the significance of Order, accountability and assessment in the ministries they are responsible for.

As you read this, the goal is not to be the conventional religious book that gives unlimited biblical and historical references, but somehow, lacks the connect-ability to make it relatable to the modern day reader. In other words, you will not have to take a graduate course in Old Testament Studies to get through this book. Teachings must make sense to the reader so they will not just hear but listen and comprehend.

Our main characters of reference will be **Moses** and **David,** and as you read this, you will need to have your Bible, I am not coming from the local newspaper. But before we get started, you need to ask yourself four questions that you will need to be able to answer by the time you have completed this book. Those questions are:

1. HAVE YOU REALLY BEEN CALLED TO MUSIC MINISTRY?

This is not a hobby. Just because you LIKE to sing, dance, preach or play an instrument...it does not mean that you have been CALLED to do it.

2. DO YOU KNOW YOUR ASSIGNMENT (AT LEAST FOR NOW) IN *YOUR CURRENT* MUSIC MINISTRY?

Do you know what your role is? Or better yet, do you even want to do the assignment that you have been given? Most music ministries are out of alignment because they are filled with two groups of people: One group does not know their assignment; The other group knows their assignment but refuse to accept it because they covet the assignment of another person.

3. ARE YOU FULLY COMMITTED?

Your assignment won't be fulfilled without commitment. You can't be seasonal in your assignment. You must remain committed through mistakes, conflict, pay reductions and personnel changes.

4. DOES YOUR DISPOSITION AND IMAGE MATCH WHO YOU ARE CALLED?

There should be a direct correlation between what your character and image are and what your name is. Not the name you were given by your parents, but the spiritual name that you are called by.

"Talent alone won't make you a success. Neither will being in the right place at the right time, unless you are ready. The most important question is: 'Are you ready?'"

Johnny Carson

SECTION I

FOUNDATION

Before you build a structure, you must lay a foundation. The building can't stand unless a proper foundation is laid. Let's take a historical look at the origins of the Levitical Priesthood.

WHAT'S IN A NAME?

"A good name is to be chosen rather than great riches, and favor is better than silver or gold."

Proverbs 22:1

In 2005, Mesha and I were blessed with the news that we would be expecting our first child. After we found out that we would have a daughter, we began to think of names. The first name that came forth was Micah. Micah is a derivative of Michael. Michael means, "At One with God." Mesha, also a derivative of Michael, means the same thing. So we were going to have a home where all of our names meant the same thing. Several months later, we had the baby shower and the name Micah appeared on all invitations mailed out, the gift bags and give-a-ways at the shower. We were excited about the arrival of Micah.

However, as we got closer to the arrival date, something interesting took place. The name changed from Micah to Mackenzie (thanks to my brother Daniel somehow constantly saying Mackenzie after he found out that was a name we were considering). Also, Mesha's father is named Mack so part of choosing Mackenzie was to honor him and we also thought the name for a girl would be special, we didn't know many African-American girls with that name. After we had changed the name, I asked if I could give her a middle name. I chose Janai' with no particular reason other than I've always liked that name. When we looked up the name Mackenzie, we found that it had an interesting meaning. The name Mackenzie means, "Leader." And when we looked up the name Janai', it means "Forgiving." And on December 30th, 2005... "The Forgiving Leader" was born into the world.

As Mackenzie Janai' began to develop language and social skills, we noticed something very interesting. She was a natural born leader. When we took her to the park or birthday parties for other children, she would always gather the children, organize & strategize play time and also put a plan together. Not only that, she was the one child in the group that had a forgiving spirit. She always settled disputes among the children, gave out hugs and forgave when another child did something to her that was wrong. She also led the "make-up" process, trying to get the children to forgive each other for fighting or arguing.

This even translated from social gatherings to the classroom. To this date, Mackenzie has had seven teachers (2 at Flossmoor Montessori, 1 in Kindergarten, 1st, 2nd, 3rd and 4th grade). All of her teachers have said the same thing to us at every parent-teacher conference, that she is the leader of the class and the peacemaker. All seven teachers have told us that they wish they could have a roomful of Mackenzie's. Now how can this be? That at such a young age, she has made such an impact on her teachers as a leader with a forgiving heart?

Every day of her life, we have called her Mackenzie Janai'. Her name means "The Forgiving Leader," we speak her name daily, and Mackenzie has had no choice but respond to whom she is called. For her disposition matches whom she is called. If the teachers had said that Mackenzie was passive and a troublemaker, then there would be some discrepancy because she is not responding to her name. We as her parents would be perplexed because who she is supposed to be is not what her disposition portrays. So the question you must ask yourself does your disposition match who you are called?

What's in a name? Let's take a look.

"I read in a book once that a rose by any other name would smell as sweet, but I've never been able to believe it. I don't believe a rose WOULD be as nice if it was called a thistle or a skunk cabbage."

L.M. Montgomery, Anne of Green Gables

THE ORIGIN OF THE NAME

Genesis 29.

Jacob has traveled to Paddan Aram, the land of the eastern peoples where his uncle Laban resides. Upon arriving in town, he comes to a well where the shepherds have gathered to water their sheep. After a brief discussion with the shepherds about the state of his uncle Laban, he looks up and sees a beautiful woman approaching the well with her sheep, for she is a shepherd also. Upon her arrival at the well, Jacob announces that he is the nephew of Laban, and he kisses her on the cheek and begins to weep. (She is that stunning).

Rachel goes and alerts her father Laban of Jacob's arrival, and they meet and talk. Jacob stays in their home for a month and after a month, Laban says to him, *"Just because you are a relative of mine, should you work for me for nothing? Tell me what your wages should be"*? Jacob is enamored with Laban's daughter so he asks for his wages from work to be Rachel's hand in marriage and says, *"I'll work for you seven years in return for your younger daughter Rachel."* Laban agrees. Jacob works, and the Bible says he loved Rachel so strongly that those seven years, *"seemed like only a few days."* (We must remember that it was not uncommon for relatives to marry one another).

After the seven years of work, Jacob demands his payment and says to Laban, *"Give me my wife. My time is completed, I want to make love to her."* Laban honors his word and arranges for the wedding of his daughter Rachel to Jacob. (During this time, wedding ceremonies were a week-long celebration. Monday through Wednesday there was a pre-wedding celebration, but at midweek, the couple consummated the marriage and after which, Thursday and Friday you continue the celebration as a married couple).

However, at midweek of the celebration, a dilemma is beginning to take shape. Laban has made a switch. Before Jacob entered the tent to consummate the marriage with his wife, Laban has taken Rachel out of the tent and replaced her with Leah. Leah was told to marry Jacob by Laban, her father, and Jacob was tricked into marrying Leah by the same man. The next morning when Jacob realized he has been tricked, confronts Laban as to why Leah was placed in the tent, he states that it was not customary for the younger daughter to marry before the oldest daughter so I replaced Rachel with her sister Leah. (After Jacob had worked the first seven years for Rachel, Leah had not been betrothed). But Laban states to Jacob that if you can complete the week of festivities, I will also give you Rachel in return for another seven years of labor. His desire and love for Rachel is so strong that he agrees. At the end of the week, he makes love to Rachel and starts his labor love. Jacob now has two wives.

In Genesis 29:[31] *"When the Lord saw that Leah was not loved, he enabled her to conceive, but Rachel remained childless. [32] Leah became pregnant and gave birth to a son. She named him Reuben, for she said, 'It is because the Lord has seen my misery. Surely my husband will love me now.'"*

One of the worse situations any human being can experience is to be in a relationship with someone who does not want you, and they are not trying because their desire is someplace else. And what makes matters worse is that they are not evil, mean or vile towards you, they simply do not desire you. Being in this situation will produce an emotion called Misery. Misery means, *"a state or feeling of great distress or discomfort of mind or body."* Misery is an emotion that has no prescribed remedy. No matter what you do, try, say, execute, it does not work. There's no pill you can take, no beverage you can drink, no act you can indulge in, no drug you can experience, no party you can attend no matter which way you turn, you are in a constant state of discomfort and distress. You are simply miserable. I can image the angst that Leah felt, the wide range of emotions that poured through her body, unresolved, as she tried and tried again to gain his heart…but Reuben did not work. He still did not love her.

Genesis 29:[33] *"She conceived again, and when she gave birth to a son she said, 'Because the Lord heard that I am not loved, he gave me this one too.' So she named him Simeon."*

How did the Lord hear? One, because I am sure Leah had been praying and talking to God about her heart's desire for her husband to love her and not love Rachel. Genesis 29:[30]…*"and his love for Rachel was greater than his love for Leah"*. But not only did God hear the concerns of Leah, but God also heard the conversations of the people because the people knew and were talking.

Today, the most popular show on TV is "Scandal". Imagine a scandal taking place over 4000 years ago and it is not something that you heard or seen someone else go through, but the character in this TV program is you. And every Thursday night at 9 pm, the world takes a pause to engulf itself in the calamity of an adulterous relationship, a love affair of a man in leadership who is torn between his lover and his wife. Now you would think we have had enough of the many secret relationships that seem to be constantly revealed in our daily lives but to no avail, Scandal draws us in. But here is the interesting thing about a scandal. Scandal is funny as long as YOU are not the character. It's cool to watch, laugh, engage in conversation and gossip about someone else's situation and mess until you are the primary actor in the production. Now can you imagine how Leah felt? Not only does her family know, but all of the people in town know, and there is nowhere she can run or hide. All the people were at the wedding. They knew Jacob had been working for Rachel. They knew Jacob's intent was to marry Rachel and not Leah, but he ended up with Leah based on a trick, but still finds it convenient to sleep with both women involved because he loves one and the other could have his children. Can you hear the talk? Whispers? Rumors? All piled on top of her misery? So the Lord heard that she was not loved, but Simeon did not work either. He still did not love her.

Genesis 29:[34] *"Again she conceived, and when she gave birth to a son she said, 'Now at last my husband will become attached to me, because I have borne him three sons.' So he was named Levi."*

The root word for Levitical is LEVI which means:

–   **TO ATTACH**

–   **JOINED TO**

–   **WE SHALL ACCOMPANY**

–   **TO PLEDGE**

Even though we have this powerful meaning and Leah was confident by proclaiming that, *"Now at last..."*, the birth of Levi did not work either. Jacob's heart was still with Rachel. We have a popular saying in western culture that says "the 3rd time's the charm" but this 3rd time didn't produce the desired result.

As I began to sit with this word "Attached" and how our Heart feels in situations like this in real life relationships and situations, I began to get a revelation. Leah was not so much concerned that her husband was having intercourse with Rachel, because Rachel was his wife also, nor was Leah's concern with the fact that Rachel was her sister, which made the situation even more scandalous. What Leah was concerned about was that Jacob's heart lay elsewhere! You are sleeping with me, but your heart is in Rachel's bed. Therefore, you are not <u>attached </u>to me. You are simply having intercourse with me.

This is why after an affair has been revealed, the first question a person asks once they have come to themselves and the emotions have settled is, "did you love them?" They asks this because if they're trying to repair the marriage and you are present with them, but your heart is in the bed of another person, reconciliation will be futile because you are <u>attached</u> to someone else.

Many marriages today don't work exactly because of the concept of attachment. The couple married but was never attached. We marry someone for companionship, but our high school sweetheart has our heart. We marry someone for financial stability, but an ex from college has our heart. We have children together, but an old co-worker has our heart. We are living together, have a mortgage or pay rent, but we are attached to someone else. We marry even in brokenness; you can't attach yourself to your spouse when your heart is still broken from a previous relationship. You are still attached to that person/relationship. So you are simply having intercourse with the person you married. And this is exactly what we do to God. God wants our heart, but we are simply having intercourse with him because our heart lies in the bed of someone or something else. God has in effect become a spiritual sugar daddy. We will give God some intercourse, (praise, worship, giving, service) when we need Him to do something for us, but He does not have our heart. God is looking for us to attach ourselves to him, not just sleep with him when we need or want Him to do something.

Many of our Priests have been guilty of manipulating the hearts of the believer, constantly preying on their emotional state by continually spinning them in a circle by misusing "Prosperity" and proclaiming God is about to do this for you…and we go into a praise. Or, if you need God to do that for you… and we go into worship. But where is the proclamation for attachment which will cause us to Obey and fall into Order? Where is the declaration for attachment which will cause us to seek Him first, (giving Him our heart) and then we will fall in Order?

So now we have the origin of the name with some context,

but when did the meaning of this name come to fruition for the Levitical Priests?

"Names have power."

Rick Riordan, The Lightning Thief

THE MANIFESTATION OF THE NAME

The Golden Calf

Exodus 32.

We are very familiar with this passage. This chapter was a key part of a historic film starring Charleston Heston called, "The Ten Commandments."

Moses went up on Mt. Sinai to spend time with the Lord and received The Commandments and while there, God spoke to Moses and told him that the children of Israel had become corrupt and began to worship an idol calf. God wanted to destroy the people, but Moses reminded God of what he promised to Abraham, Isaac and the children of Israel and God repented, or changed His mind.

As Moses returned down to camp, Joshua commented to Moses in verse 17 that, "*There is the sound of war in the camp.*" But Moses, who was acutely familiar with what war sounded like replied in verse 18 that, "*It is not the sound of victory, it is not the sound of defeat; it is the sound of singing that I hear.*"

As Moses and Joshua entered the camp, [25] "*Moses saw that the people were running wild and that Aaron had let them get out of control and so become a laughingstock to their enemies.* ²⁶ *So he stood at the entrance to the camp and said, 'Whoever is for the Lord, come to me.' And all the Levites rallied to him."*

²⁹ Then Moses said, "*This is what the LORD, THE GOD OF ISRAEL, SAYS: 'EACH MAN STRAP A SWORD TO HIS SIDE. GO BACK AND FORTH THROUGH THE CAMP FROM ONE END TO THE OTHER, EACH KILLING HIS BROTHER AND FRIEND AND NEIGHBOR.'" ²⁸ The Levites did as Moses commanded, and that day about three thousand of the people died. ²⁹ Then Moses said, "You have been set apart to the LORD TODAY, FOR YOU WERE AGAINST YOUR OWN SONS AND BROTHERS, AND HE HAS BLESSED YOU THIS DAY."*

Why did God choose the Levites to be the one tribe He set apart for Himself in a special way? The Levites did just as they were commanded, and slaughtered 3,000 people in one day. That finally got the camp's attention, and the people settled down. This was an act of obedience and atonement for the sins of idolatry that the people committed. This act of obedience showed God that the Levites were willing to slaughter brother, friend, and neighbor for Him.

The meaning of your name came forth in Genesis 29, but the manifestation of your name came forth several hundred years later in Exodus 32 when you, the Levites finally attached yourself, you pledged yourself, you joined. That which did not take place between Leah and Jacob took place between you and the Lord. When you choose, God set us apart for service. Levitical Priests, this is key. Are you willing, even when in error, to atone and pledge yourself to God?

"...go in the direction your head is pointed in."

Jung Chang, Wild Swans: Three Daughters of China

Because we were <u>set apart</u> for service after we pledged ourselves to the Lord under Moses, we were given unique assignments that could only be carried out by the Levitical priests. Let's identify those specific roles/assignments that we gained during this time.

<u>Assignment 1</u>

Numbers 3:5-6,⁵ The Lord said to Moses, ⁶ *"Bring the tribe of Levi and present them to Aaron the priest to <u>assist him</u>."*

<u>Assignment 2</u>

Number 3:7-8,⁷ *"They are to perform duties for him and for the whole community at the tent of meeting by <u>doing the work of the tabernacle</u>. ⁸ They are to take care of all the furnishings of the tent of meeting, fulfilling the obligations of the Israelites by doing the work of the tabernacle. "*

<u>Assignment 3</u>

Deuteronomy 10:8, ⁸ *"At that time the LORD set apart the tribe of Levi to <u>carry the ark of the covenant of the LORD</u>, to stand before the LORD to minister and to pronounce blessings in his name, as they still do today."*

The Levites received three distinct and special assignments directly from God during the time of Moses once the Levites attached themselves to Him. *(The marching orders for the Levites and Children of Israel for battle and for transporting the Ark can be seen in Chart 1).*

Assignment 1: To assist, what does this mean for us today? Whenever there is a service that takes place in the tabernacle, Levites must be present to assist the Pastor in the delivering of the Word of God. There should never be a time when a service is going on, and there is no Levites present. You cannot assist when you are not available.

Assignment 2: To do the work of the tabernacle, what does this mean for us today? First, we are to make sure the tabernacle is physically prepared for worship. Instruments, sound, wardrobe, banners, tapestry, blessed oil, communion, etc. should all be ready before the tabernacle doors are opened. But this is deeper than simply making sure the tabernacle is physically prepared, this also means we must have ourselves spiritually prepared so that when we enter the tabernacle, the work can be done. We must make sure our spirit is prepared by prayer. Have we made a sacrifice to the Lord by walking in obedience? 1 Samuel 15:[22] *"Does the LORD delight in burnt offerings and sacrifices as much as in obeying the voice of the LORD? To obey is better than sacrifice, and to heed is better than the fat of rams."* We cannot effectively do the work of the tabernacle while walking in disobedience. And finally, have we offered ourselves? Romans 12:1-2 *"Therefore, I urge you, brothers and sisters, in view of God's mercy, to offer your bodies as a living sacrifice, holy and pleasing to God—this is your true and proper worship."*

Assignment 3: To carry the ark of the covenant of the Lord, what does this mean for us today? As Levitical priests, we have to assume the task of carrying or handling and accompanying God's anointing. Through song, dance, singing, speaking...we usher in God's presences.

> *"Always render more and better service than is expected of you, no matter what your task may be."*
>
> Og Mandino

LEVITICAL CHARACTERISTICS

The Mosaic Era

Moses was a Levite. The descendant from Amram; descendant of Kohath; descendant of Levi, who was the son of Jacob. And there are certain characteristics that Moses possessed that should be present among those that are called to be Levites that we must possess. Let's take a look at those.

Moses Prepared a Successor

Exodus 24:[12] *"The Lord said to Moses, 'Come up to me on the mountain and stay here, and I will give you the tablets of stone with the law and commandments I have written for their instruction.'"*

[13] *"Then Moses set out with Joshua his aide, and Moses went up on the mountain of God. [14] He said to the elders, "Wait here for us until we come back to you."*

- Levites identify and train someone to take your place and bring them along with you. You must have this person as an aide, assisting you, experiencing and seeing the things that you see so that when it is time for them to lead, they will be prepared. Moses here took Joshua up to the mountain with him. Levites in their preparation are not secretive or withholding to the person(s) that will succeed them.

Numbers 27:[16] *"May the* LORD, THE GOD *WHO GIVES BREATH TO ALL LIVING THINGS, APPOINT SOMEONE OVER THIS COMMUNITY* [17] *to go out and come in before them, one who will lead them out and bring them in, so the* LORD'S *PEOPLE WILL NOT BE LIKE SHEEP WITHOUT A SHEPHERD."* [18] *So the* LORD *SAID TO* MOSES, *"TAKE* JOSHUA *SON OF* NUN, *A MAN IN WHOM IS THE SPIRIT OF LEADERSHIP, AND* <u>*lay your hand on him.*</u> [19] *Have him stand before Eleazar the priest and* <u>*the entire assembly and commission him in their presence.*</u> [20] *Give him some of your authority so the whole Israelite community will obey him."*

- Here you see that there was a transferring of authority and ordainment when the appointed time came. Moses didn't die in his position and let chaos take place among the people with no shepherd set in place to lead them. He did as the Lord commanded, and set Joshua in place <u>openly</u> so that the people will follow and obey him. But also, notice that the Bible says Joshua had a spirit of leadership in him already...we will get into that later.

Still Served after Judgment

In Numbers 20:[8], *"the Lord told Moses, 'Take the staff, and you and your brother Aaron gather the assembly together. Speak to that rock before their eyes and it will pour out its water. You will bring water out of the rock for the community so they and their livestock can drink".* Numbers 20:[9-11] records Moses' response: *"So Moses took the staff from the LORD's presence, just as He commanded him. He and Aaron* *gathered the assembly together in front of the rock and Moses said to them, 'Listen, you rebels, must **we** bring you water out of this rock?' Then Moses raised his arm and struck the rock twice with his staff. Water gushed out, and the community and their livestock drank"*. The Lord was displeased with Moses' actions and in verse 12 *"Because you did not trust in me enough to honor me as holy in the sight of the Israelites, you will not bring this community into the land I give them"*.

What did Moses do that warranted such a severe penalty from the Lord? First, Moses disobeyed a direct command from God. God had commanded Moses to speak to the rock. Instead, Moses struck the rock with his staff. Second, Moses took the credit for bringing forth the water. Notice how in verse 10 Moses says, *"Must **we** [referring to Moses and Aaron] bring you water out of this rock?"* Moses took credit for the miracle himself, instead of attributing it to God. Third, Moses committed this sin in front of all the Israelites. Such a public example of direct disobedience could not go unpunished. But what we DO know is that Moses did not quit and return to Egypt, he did not blame God, he did not leave the Israelites he served alone. So the questions for you are:

- Will you still serve if your pay is reduced?

- Will you still serve if you are no longer the director?

- Will you still serve if you are not called on?

- Will you still serve if you are replaced?

Now, let me qualify this. This does not give the Priest or ministry leader ANY right to mistreat you or mishandle you in any way. But if things are done decently and in Order, a change in status should not cause you to give up serving.

Settled Disputes

Exodus 18:[15] *"Moses answered him, 'Because the people come to me to seek God's will.* [16] *Whenever they have a dispute, it is brought to me, and I decide between the parties and inform them of God's decrees and instructions.'"*

- Levites settle disputes; they refrain from discord, and they address conflict. Levites do not take pleasure in situations being combative and unresolved. Levites like order, resolution and refrain from messy situations.

Listens to wise counsel

Exodus18:[13] *"The next day Moses took his seat to serve as judge for the people, and they stood around him from morning till evening.* [14] *When his father-in-law saw all that Moses was doing for the people, he said, "What is this you are doing for the people? Why do you alone sit as judge, while all these people stand around you from morning till evening?'*

[17] *"Moses' father-in-law replied, 'What you are doing is not good.* [18] *You and these people who come to you will only wear yourselves out. The work is too heavy for you; you cannot handle it alone.* [19] *Listen now to me and I will give you some advice, and may God be with you. You must be the people's representative before God and bring their disputes to him.* [20] *Teach them his decrees and instructions, and show them the way they are to live and how they are to behave".* And in verse 24, it says, *"Moses listened to his father-in-law and did everything he said."*

- Here Jethro, the father-in-law of Moses pays him a visit and sees that Moses is completely overwhelmed with his leadership assignment and sees that this is not good, so he offers him some advice that benefited Moses without hindering the people he served. And in verse 24 it states that *"Moses listened..."*. Levites listen and take heed to wise counsel; we do not get combative when people come to offer advice that will only help us carry out our assignment more effectively.

Does not do all the work

Exodus 18:²¹-*"But select capable men from all the people—men who fear God, trustworthy men who hate dishonest gain—and appoint them as officials over thousands, hundreds, fifties and tens. ²² Have them serve as judges for the people at all times, but have them bring every difficult case to you; the simple cases they can decide themselves. That will make your load lighter, because they will share it with you".*

- Jethro again, in giving him wise counsel, advises him on what type of leaders Moses should select to help him carry the load. Levites do not take pleasure in doing all the work themselves and seek help. The sheer weight of the assignment requires help from capable men and women. They realize, either initially or with counsel that the assignment cannot be carried by one person alone.

Has seen God

Exodus 33:¹⁸ *"Then Moses said, 'Now show me your glory.'"* ¹⁹ *And the Lord said, 'I will cause all my goodness to pass in front of you, and I will proclaim my name, the Lord, in your presence. I will have mercy on whom I will have mercy, and I will have compassion on whom I will have compassion.'* [20] *But, he said, 'you cannot see my face, for no one may see me and live.'* [21] *Then the Lord said, 'There is a place near me where you may stand on a rock.* [22] *When my glory passes by, I will put you in a cleft in the rock and cover you with my hand until I have passed by.* [23] *Then I will remove my hand and you will see my back; but my face must not be seen.'"*

- Levites have spent time alone (intimately) with God. They know who God is because they have a personal relationship with him away from their responsibilities in the Tabernacle and away from the masses. Moses was effective because he knew God AWAY from his assignments with and for the people. Do you spend time with God AWAY from your ministry responsibilities?

7. Consults God

Numbers 9:[8] *"Moses answered them, 'Wait until I find out what the Lord commands concerning you.'"*

- In this passage, there was an issue raised concerning what to do about the Passover. Some of the Israelites had become ceremonially unclean due to a dead body. Instead of Moses making a personal decision on what he felt should be done, Moses addressed the people and said that before any decision is made, I will consult the Lord. Levites consult God before major decisions, especially those that require a spiritual response, are made.

So what has taken place in today's music ministry? Because we fail to identify people who have these Levitical traits as we saw under Moses, we have put the wrong people in position. And because of this we have allowed the Temple to get out of Order, and it remains unfixed. How do we resolve this issue? We must take a look at these four areas:

"Be more concerned with your character than your reputation, because your character is what you really are, while your reputation is merely what others think you are."

John Wooden

SECTION II
STRUCTURE

We have completed Section I where the foundation was laid to give you some historical perspective on the Levitical Priesthood origins. Now, let's begin to discuss some structural topics so that the music ministry can be built.

PLAN

"Then the Lord replied: 'Write down the revelation and make it plain on tablets so that a herald may run with it.'"

Habakkuk 2:2

For years, we have misinterpreted this scripture. What we must realize is that a vision is NOT a dream... it's a PLAN. Our Levitical leaders fail because they accept a position with no plan in the works, no plan in hand and no thoughts on developing a plan. The works of God and the work of the temple will not be accomplished without a Plan.

When you have a plan (vision or revelation), and it is written down, it holds you accountable to it because there is a reference point. When it is written, and it is made plain, then it becomes understandable to the (herald or the person or people) who will read it and be responsible for carrying it out. When the plan is understandable, then it is executable (that a herald may run with it).

So you must have a Plan…that is written for accountability.

The Plan must be made plain…so that the people will understand it.

When the plan is understandable…then it is executable.

Anything that is executable…brings results.

Let's take a look at David under the execution of a Plan.

1 Chronicles 28:[13] *"He gave him instructions for the divisions of the priests and Levites, and for all the work of serving in the temple of the Lord, as well as for all the articles to be used in its service."*

[19] *"All this," David said, "I have in writing as a result of the Lord's hand on me, and he enabled me to understand all the details of the plan."*

We know that David was not permitted to build the Temple, his son Solomon received that honor. But David received the instructions for the plan and it was in writing so that those that labored on the construction of the Temple and those that would serve in the Temple, once completed, could execute their assignment. Nothing in the music ministry will be successful without first a plan of construction, implementation and execution for it.

The modern day church should be following a Davidic model/ plan for music ministry. The books of 1 and 2 Chronicles should be read thoroughly so that you can gain perspective and insight on how David structured and planned music ministry in the temple. What is this David model? The worship of the Tabernacle of David focused on the presence of the Lord in the midst of his people. The Davidic model/worshiper offered a *"sacrifice of praise to God- the fruit of lips that acknowledge his name."* As stated in Hebrews 13:15. The Davidic Model was a blend of prescribed structure and improvised expression. It was conducted by priests who were skilled singers and instrumentalists. The temple became a worship center under David, Psalms 122:[1] *"I rejoiced with those who said to me, "Let us go to the house of the Lord."[2] Our feet are standing in your gates, Jerusalem.[3] Jerusalem is built like a city that is closely compacted together.[4] That is where the tribes go up—the tribes of the Lord—to praise the name of the Lord according to the statute given to Israel."* There should be celebration, expression, demonstration, and manifestation in the temple of the Lord. A manifest presence of the Lord should be experienced through music, singing, dancing and declaration (speaking). This is the essence of the David model.

There is something even more interesting to notice here in 1 Chronicles 28:19 David said, *"I have in writing as a result of the Lord's hand on me."* David just didn't receive a plan from a friend. He didn't observe what another kingdom was doing in another part of the world and copied it. However, David received his plan from the Lord. The Lord's hand was on him, meaning he was anointed, had a relationship with God and the instructions for the building of the temple came directly from Him. Make sure that the plan you develop for the music ministry comes from the Lord as a result of His hand being upon you. You consult God, and his anointing and glory rests on you.

"A goal without a plan is just a wish."

Antoine de Saint-Exupéry

WRONG PLAN...WILL FOLLOW

"If a ruler listens to falsehood, all his officials will be wicked."

Proverbs 29:12

D o you know that having a plan is so important that people will follow you even if what you are saying is wrong if you have a plan? Let's take a look at a natural example of this.

On 1 April 1924, a young man was sentenced to five years' imprisonment at Landsberg Prison for leading an unsuccessful revolt in the state of Bavaria. He hoped that his nationalist revolution in Bavaria would spread to the dissatisfied army, which in turn would bring down the government that was not able to turn the country around after WWI. However, the uprising was immediately suppressed. While at Landsberg, this man wrote a book entitled, *Mein Kampf* (*My Struggle*), this book was an autobiography and exposition of his ideology. *Mein Kampf* laid out plans for transforming a society into one based on race. Passages included genocide, 1000-year reign, and racial superiority. After nine months, The Bavarian Supreme Court issued a pardon, and he was released from jail on 20 December 1924. After his release, he published the book in two volumes in 1925 and 1926, and it sold 228,000 copies between 1925 and 1932. One million copies were sold in 1933 alone.

In 1932, this man ran against Paul Von Hindenburg, who was currently the President, in the presidential elections. And he came in second in both rounds of the election, garnering more than 35 percent of the vote in the final election. Although he lost to Hindenburg, this election established him as a strong force in politics.

As time went on, the absence of an effective government as well as his ability to deliver powerful public speeches, prompted two influential politicians, Franz von Papen and Alfred Hugenberg, along with several other industrialists and businessmen, to write a letter to Hindenburg. The signers urged Hindenburg to appoint this man as leader of the government "independent from parliamentary parties," which could turn into a movement that would "enrapture millions of people."

Hindenburg reluctantly agreed to appoint him as chancellor after two further parliamentary elections—in July and November 1932—had not resulted in the formation of a majority government. He later gained power and authority to push policy through the Enabling Act and in 1934, President Hindenburg died and left the door open for this man to take full control. Do you know who this man was? Adolf Hitler. Hitler's appointment to Chancellor paved the way for the German government and all its officials to become wicked and ignited the flame for WWII.

Hitler's selection as Chancellor of Germany was sparked by a book he wrote while in prison, detailing a plan for Germany that included genocide, racial supremacy, and world domination. The people who elected him knew of the book, had read the book, but even though the contents of the book were morally, socially, and legally wrong, he was still chosen as chancellor because he had a Plan. No other candidate that ran for President of Germany had a written plan to counter Adolf Hitler. So he was essentially elected uncontested.

Even in today's elections, no presidential candidate is nominated to represent their prospective party, let alone elected as President of the United States of America without some form of a Plan written and presented to their constituents and voters. A plan is essential to the success of the Levitical Priest, who is in the position of leadership and supervision. You cannot move the ministry forward, nor repair it, without a Plan.

"No enemy is worse than bad advice"

Sophocles

THE ARCHITECT

"Strategic planning is the key to warfare; to win, you need a lot of good counsel."

Proverbs 24:6

In 1994, God gave me the exact position that I wanted to have after graduation from Northern Illinois University. I had been working as an Academic Advisor at Moraine Valley Community College for two years and in 1996, a position was created entitled, Coordinator of Minority Student Achievement that would be housed in the Minority Student Transfer Center. This was a brand new role sparked by a movement at colleges and universities around the country to address the growing concerns of minority recruitment, retention, and graduation from institutions of higher learning. I was given the position, and it made me the youngest African-American male administrator in the State of Illinois at the time. Before my announcement to the college on my appointment in this new capacity, the President (Emeritus) of the college, Dr. Vernon Crawley, sent me an emailing inviting me into his office for a discussion. He expressed that he wanted to give me a word of advice. I must admit; I had never been in a President's Office before. However, I felt like I belonged as if I was talking to a King, who had summoned one of his officials for a very important assignment. Dr. Crawley was a large, fair-skinned African-American man who had a doctorate in Chemistry, highly intelligent and great at forming alliances. As I entered his office, I sat down and concentrated every ounce of being in me to be as attentive as possible. Because, as I observed him over the years, he was a man that rarely spent much time in small talk, he sat back in his chair and began to speak these words, *"An architect never builds off an unfinished blueprint."*

This simple but direct comment to me told me all I needed to know about my new position. Dr. Crawley was telling me that you will not be successful in this new position without a completed plan. Dr. Crawley was also telling me that if I start with an unfinished blueprint, those that work for and with me in my department will never be able to complete any initiatives, projects or assignments that fall under this position and I will lose the respect of those other administrators who work alongside me.

When you process this even further, this is exactly what an architect does. Before any construction on a building takes place, the blueprints are already completed, the architect is working from the end to the beginning, and the laborers are working from the beginning to the end. The architect already knows what that building will look like, how it will function, the dimensions, the time frame to completion and its capacity, because he possesses the blueprint (plan) in hand. Even as pedestrians and onlookers travel by the construction zone and can't formulate a picture in their minds of how this project will turn out. The architect knows

46

because he is in possession of a completed plan.

As a Levitical leader, you must possess, in hand, the plan for what that music ministry will look like, how it will function, the scope and dimensions and your time frame to completion and you must guide those that will occupy and serve towards the details (construction) of the plan.

Before I was announced as Team Lead of Music and Fine Arts Ministry at VKMI, I spent six months developing a plan. After which came, a 70-page manifesto which simply means *"a public declaration or **document** of intentions, opinions, objectives, or motives, as one issued by a government, sovereign, organization or candidate."* Simply put a Plan.

After you have your plan/blueprint written and a detailed understanding of it, you must look at how you will convey this plan to those that you lead so that construction can take place or as Habakkuk says, *"so they may run with it."* Let's take a look at some ways to assist them in running with it.

> *"Start with the end in mind."*
>
> *Stephen R. Covey*

HOW DO YOU TEACH?

"A disciple is not above his teacher, but everyone when he is fully trained will be like his teacher."

Luke 6:40

I worked in higher education for 14 years at four different colleges and universities working in areas of advising to recruitment. One of the positions I had was Director of Articulation, Assessment, and Curriculum. This was a very intense position, working with both faculty and high-level administrators. Whereas at most colleges and universities, this position is broken down into three different departments and persons. At this particular institution, these areas were housed under one department with one person…ME.

Under the area of Curriculum, I worked with faculty on creating new curriculum, enhancing existing curriculum and deleting old curriculum that students no longer were interested in, or the workforce no longer had a need for. One of the most important things I learned while in this position was understanding the importance and impact of the <u>Teaching Method</u> of the instructor and the <u>Learning Style</u> of the student. This falls under the area of Assessment and Evaluation.

According to, Assessment of Student Learning in STEM disciplines, a Duke University 'Teaching IDEAS Workshop' presented by Ed Neal, Ph.D. Director of Faculty Development, Center for Teaching and Learning, University of North Carolina, Assessment *focuses on learning, teaching, and outcomes. It provides information for improving learning and teaching. Assessment is an interactive process between students and faculty that informs faculty how well their students are learning what they are teaching. The information is used by faculty to make changes in the learning environment and is shared with students to assist them in improving their learning and study habits.*

In education, there are four main categories of Teaching Methods. They are:

Explaining– Lecture

The process of teaching by giving spoken explanations of the subject that is to be learned.

Demonstrating– Teaching

The process of teaching through examples or experiments.

Collaborating–Teacher/Student

The process of actively allowing students to participate in the learning process by talking with each other and listening to other points of view. Collaborating establishes a personal connection between the student and the topic of study.

Learning by Teaching-Peer Teaching

The process of allowing the student to assume the role of teacher and teach their peers. Students who teach others as a group or individual must study and understand a topic well enough to teach it to their peers.

We can't talk about teaching methods without discussing learning styles.

There are three <u>main</u> categories of Learning Styles. They are:

Visual

The student learns by seeing and looking. (*observation*)

Auditory

The student learns by hearing and listening. (*teaching*)

Kinesthetic

The student learns by touching and doing. (*instruction*)

One of the most important hires a Pastor of a church will make is...who will lead the music ministry. The music department tends to not only be the largest ministry in a church but the most influential. Music is a drawing card in that not only does it attract people to visit and attend church, but it also allows the congregation to comprehend the Word of God in a different format. Many times the congregation may not grasp or accept the auditory Word of God; however, they can and will accept and adhere more quickly to the Word of God presented in a lyrical and melodic format. Music is like an assist in basketball. The pass has to be made at the right time, in the right way for the shooter to have a chance at making the basket. The music assists the preacher in bringing the congregation together. Anthony Storr, in his book *Music and the Mind*, stresses that in all societies, "*a primary function of music is collective and communal, to bring and bind people together. Our auditory systems, our nervous systems, are tuned for music. Perhaps we are a musical species no less than a linguistic one*". Music has the ability to be more powerful than what you say and speak.

Many times, Pastors make the mistake of looking more at name recognition, degrees, playing or singing ability, resume and credentials and even now, the lifestyle of the individual. Which you should look at all these areas before making a decision. However, what they tend to fail to spend much time pondering is, does this potential minister of music, choir, dance or music director, worship leader, etc., teach the way the people they will instruct, learn. Frequently, Pastors match the wrong teacher with the student and this causes development, enhancement, and learning not to take place. Pastors, you must ask yourself, am I actively, consistently, and measurably assessing the music ministry to make sure initiatives in the plan (outcomes) are met.

What you find in education in many instances when students are failing, it's not that the student can't learn, does not want to learn or that the teacher is incompetent, does not care or needs more training. What has simply happened is Administration has not made the proper evaluations and have placed the wrong teacher in the wrong classroom. The students don't learn (construct) because the learning style of the student does not connect with the teaching method of the instructor. Therefore, the educational institution does not meet the initiatives (outcomes) of the Plan prescribed by the State Board and/or District Administration. The same happens in music ministry.

Pastors and music administrators, make sure you know <u>How</u> your music ministry members learn, especially if there is no plan to replace the existing members, then make the correct hire to put the correct instructor with them.

The worship leader may be anointed to sing, but not instruct, or may be too advanced for the members/learners you currently have in that ministry; this will hinder the plan. Or the reverse may be taking place. Your members/learners may be too advanced for the worship leader/teacher so there is nothing they can learn from them; this will hinder the plan.

Now, in doing your evaluation, you must be careful. People can and will use this as an excuse to complain to get rid of leaders who are effective, that they not like or care for. Have discernment so that you can know if this is personal so that you do not get rid of the right person for the ministry. The point is to <u>assess</u>, then make the correct match that the plan/blueprint can be conveyed (made plain) in the correct way so that it is constructed (run with it) and produce results in the music ministry. So ask yourself, what are you teaching? What are the ministry members learning? Are they meeting the projected outcomes?

Evaluation, *focuses on grades and may reflect classroom components other than course content and mastery level. These could include discussion, cooperation, attendance, and verbal ability.* Not only must you assess the learning environment, but you must <u>evaluate</u> those that have been selected in the classroom (music ministry).

Now we do not give report cards in the church, however, what are you as Pastors and Music Ministry leaders using to evaluate those that you have selected to be Levitical priests? There should be some rubric or evaluation method developed to assess your team. Do they come to Bible study or service when they are NOT on the schedule? Has there been any spiritual growth? Have they been delivered from those things that had them bound? Have you observed improvements in their disposition and character? Or is the only evaluation being done is if the music sounds good and looks good while in the pulpit, on instruments, in the choir stand or behind the sacred desk? There must be a constant evaluation process. There must be evaluation infused into your plan for the music ministry. If not, you have no way of measurably knowing if things are improving.

"The mediocre teacher tells. The good teacher explains. The superior teacher demonstrates. The great teacher inspires."

William Arthur Ward

TIPS FOR PLAN

- <u>Do not reinvent the wheel</u>

  Use the Bible as your template. It's the blueprint. It works if you follow it.

- <u>Seek Advice</u>

  This is so important to your development of a plan. You must seek out those that have been and are successful leaders of ministry in your area, region or the country. Wise counsel will be one of your biggest allies...once you seek...listen.

- <u>Scout</u>

  Identify other churches that are similar to yours that are effective at producing results and observe what they are doing and incorporate what may work in your ministry.

- <u>Budget</u>

  Finances are key, know what is allocated for your ministry and know how much wiggle room you have to maneuver thru the calendar year. You should have a solid relationship with Administration and Finance departments of the church.

- ## Calendar

  The calendar is your friend. A calendar has <u>foresight</u> because it allows you to look (plan) ahead. Find out what events during the year must be staffed by the music ministry and incorporate that into a master calendar. Also, build the music ministry calendar out as far in advance as you can, even if you have to modify it later. Never operate from week to week.

- ## Complete

  Complete your plan BEFORE you are introduced as the leader, even if your announcement has to be delayed and enhance the plan as you go. Complete all projects and initiatives. See them through.

- ## Convey

  Present the plan to the pastor and other music ministry leaders for input and support. You are in your position to serve the Priest. And present the plan to the ministry members once it is approved. A plan won't work under insurrection and mutiny from those you lead due to lack of communication.

- ## Collaborate

  You need allies. Your plan will not work without collaboration from adjacent ministries that you must work and interact with. Meet with other ministry leaders to see how the music ministry can help them in their endeavors. *"Dr. Jerry Buss was smart. Dr. Buss said, 'I'm going to get the best dude, [Jerry West], to help me achieve my goals. Then I will get the best coach [Phil Jackson]. Jim Buss got to quit trying to prove a point to everyone that he can do it on his own and just say, let me get someone beside me to help achieve the goals I want*"-Magic Johnson (in response to the L.A. Lakers problems in 2013). In developing your plan, you have to realize that you first must get out of your own way and get the best people who can actually help. You can't do it alone!

- Correct

  Don't live with a mistake, correct it. Don't allow pride to cause you to work in error. People that are successful were never afraid to re-examine or make adjustments to the original blueprint before and during construction. Remember, you are envisioning the final product, never erect mistakes, if it doesn't fit remove and replace.

- Measure

  Assess and Evaluate. Always have a rubric (a form of measurement) built into your plan. Whether doing evaluation by qualitative means, which is knowledge/information gained through observation combined with interpretative understanding such as 1-on-1 meetings or by quantitative means which is by gathering data and information that can be measured such as attendance it must be done.

- ONLY serve leaders who believe in the Plan

  The founder of FedEx, Frederick W. Smith, while in college at Yale University in 1962, wrote a paper on "Outlining Overnight Delivery Service in a Computer Information Age." His professor told him, "*in order for you to get a C grade, the idea has to be feasible.*" So the professor gave him an "F" on the paper. FedEx is now the largest delivery company in the world and revenues in 2012 were 42 billion, after taxes. FedEx makes more money than the U.S. Postal Service. The professor never believed in him. Never work, serve or sit under anyone who doubts the plan.

When you have an effective Plan, then you can begin to set things in Order. You cannot have Order without a Plan. And Order is not what you may normally think that it is…let's take a look.

ORDER

*"Put your outdoor work in order and get your fields ready;
after that, build your house."*

Proverbs 24:27

Order is defined as, *the arrangement or disposition of people
or things in relation to each other according to a particular
sequence, pattern, or method. Synonyms include: sequence, arrangement,
organization, disposition, system, series, and succession.*

Songs are not simply written; they are arranged and sequenced.
Songs have an intro, verse, chorus, bridge, vamp and outro and
sometimes a reprise. Songs have organization. And the same must
hold true to the music ministry.

Order is not telling people what to do or being the boss or
having a title. Order deals with <u>Assignments</u>. Where there is a
lack of assignments, there is no Order. When there is Order, then
the Levites have assignments. Just like the song is arranged and
sequenced, the people involved with the song have an assignment

to make sure that the song is interpreted correctly. One of the reasons many music departments are not successful is because there is no Order. No one knows what their assignment is; there are no defined roles, and there is no Standard Operating Procedure (S.O.P) in place. This leads to the music ministry being unorganized and chaotic. Let's look at the beginnings of Order under Moses.

Numbers 1:[50] *"Instead, appoint the Levites to be in charge of the tabernacle of the covenant law—over all its furnishings and everything belonging to it. They are to carry the tabernacle and all its furnishings; they are to take care of it and encamp around it. [51] Whenever the tabernacle is to move, the Levites are to take it down, and whenever the tabernacle is to be set up, the Levites shall do it. Anyone else who approaches it is to be put to death. [52] The Israelites are to set up their tents by divisions, each of them in their own camp under their standard. [53] The Levites, however, are to set up their tents around the tabernacle of the covenant law so that my wrath will not fall on the Israelite community. The Levites are to be responsible for the care of the tabernacle of the covenant law."*

Here, the Levites received their assignments. The Levites knew, beforehand, what their role would be from the leader.

Numbers 18:[2] *"Bring your fellow Levites from your ancestral tribe to join you and assist you when you and your sons minister before the tent of the covenant law. [3] They are to be responsible to you and are to perform all the duties of the tent, but they must not go near the furnishings of the sanctuary or the altar. Otherwise both they and you will die. [4] They are to join you and be responsible for the care of the tent of meeting—all the work at the tent—and no one else may come near where you are. [5] "You are to be responsible for the care of the sanctuary and the altar, so that my wrath will not fall on the Israelites again. ⁶ I myself have selected your fellow Levites from among the Israelites as a gift to you, dedicated to the Lord to do the work at the tent of meeting."*

Here you see the word "responsible." You cannot be responsible for something if you have not been assigned to it. And you cannot properly complete an assignment without care for it. Do you care about the assignment you have been given? Do you care if it is done in excellence and executed to the best of your ability? Do you require excellence from those that labor with you?

Let's shift to the time of David and the assignments given to the Levites.

1 Chronicles 23:¹ *"When David was old and full of years, he made his son Solomon king over Israel.² He also gathered together all the leaders of Israel, as well as the priests and Levites. ³ The Levites thirty years old or more were counted, and the total number of men was thirty-eight thousand. ⁴ David said, 'Of these, twenty-four thousand are to be in charge of the work of the temple of the Lord and six thousand are to be officials and judges. ⁵ Four thousand are to be gatekeepers and four thousand are to praise the Lord with the musical instruments I have provided for that purpose.'"*

Here David gives clear directive to the Levites on their assignments in the Temple.

But in addition to having assignments for the Levites as a whole, you can't have Order without having Gatekeepers. And this is the topic within Order that I want to spend some time on. It's easy to talk about the assignment of the singers, musicians, dancers, elders, and ministers, etc. But we need to look more closely at the

Gatekeepers.

1 Chronicles 9:[22] *"Altogether, those chosen to be gatekeepers at the thresholds numbered 212. They were registered by genealogy in their villages. The gatekeepers had been <u>assigned</u> to their positions of trust by David and Samuel the seer.* [23] *They and their descendants were in charge of <u>guarding the gates</u> of the house of the Lord—the house called the tent of meeting.* [24] *The gatekeepers were on the four sides: east, west, north and south.* [25] *Their fellow Levites in their villages had to come from time to time and share their duties for seven-day periods."*

During the time of David, these 212 who were chosen from 4000 gatekeepers as previously mentioned in 1 Chronicles 23, assumed the responsibilities of policing the Temple and guarding the outer gates, the tent of meeting and the storehouse, day and night. If a leper or anyone who had defiled the temple had entered into the Temple area or any Priest officiated in a state of uncleanliness would be killed. These gatekeepers had the responsibility for security, both in a practical and spiritual sense. They made sure that only those who were ready (cleansed) to serve and worship God could enter into the temple and its associated buildings. Their work had to be organized and arranged just as much as the work of the priests who officiated at the sacrifices. Let's look at this more in-depth and in relation to today.

When I accepted the position with VKMI in 2010, before I was announced, the first meeting I had was not with the musicians, singers or dancers or the choir or praise team or administration to see what my budget would be. It was with a ministry called Tephillia or the Gatekeepers/Intercessors. The gatekeepers, in this New Testament model for the music ministry, represent the

Intercessors whose assignment is that of guarding the gates. You cannot have an effective music ministry that will accomplish its assignments without forming an alliance with the prayer and intercessor ministry. The prayer and intercessor ministry is one that is assigned to spiritually guard the gate of the temple to make sure that it is not infiltrated by unclean spirits.

During the time of David, the gatekeepers assumed the responsibilities of policing the Temple and guarding the outer gates and the storehouse, day and night. (*Part of some of the gatekeeper's assignments included guarding the treasuries, but it was more than that*). The laws of Levitical cleanness were most rigidly enforced upon worshippers and priests. If a leper or anyone who was defiled had entered into the Temple area or any priest officiated in a state of uncleanness he would, if discovered, be dragged out and killed. Now, of course, we cannot drag anyone out physically to be killed, but all unclean and contaminating spirits need to be identified up front and eliminated before they have an opportunity to enter into the Temple. If not, what happens is those spirits will take root and manifest in the Temple and pull the Levitical priests off their assignment and the Temple will be overrun and destroyed from within by its Levitical members.

We see this happen at many Temples today, the praise team, choir, music staff, ministerial and prophetic teams that work alongside the music ministry are destroyed from within because they allowed people into the ministry that should not have been admitted or hired. And they bring unclean spirits with them that take root in the group, causing division and insurrection, and this takes place because no one was assigned to guard the gates or they were pulled off the gates. Even in your audition and selection process, a gatekeeper should be present.

How are gatekeepers pulled from their assignment of guarding the gate? By being pulled away from the gate by petty skirmishes that take place inside the Temple among the Levitical Priests. Settling arguments, issues, conflicts that are minor inside the Temple for prolonged periods of time pulls gatekeepers away from this vital assignment. So unclean and perverse spirits, then become free to walk through the gates. This is why it is vital for deliverance to take place before people are formally admitted. Strongholds that people have not overcome can manifest themselves and multiply in a ministry if unchecked or not seen. Not settling conflicts and problems quickly before they are allowed to manifest causes the music ministry to become unstable.

The assignment of the gatekeeper is extremely vital, but what we often see is not many people want to be a gatekeeper/intercessor because this position does not bring glory. It does not bring popularity; it does not bring you to the forefront. Your name is not called before men; you are not celebrated in this position. It is an in the trenches and down and dirty position that requires warfare. The gatekeepers are a "front line" assignment that enables the music ministry to fulfill its assignment.

Not only must gatekeepers be established and assigned, but You must also have Standard Operating Procedures (S.O.P) under the area of Order. Procedure is defined as, "*an established or official way of doing something*". In the time of Moses, God sets a procedure for the Levitical Priests. Let's take a look.

Numbers 8:[14] *"In this way you are to set the Levites apart from the other Israelites, and the Levites will be mine.* [15] *"After you have purified the Levites and presented them as a wave offering, they are to come to do their work at the tent of meeting.* [16] *They are the Israelites who are to be given wholly to me. I have taken them as my own in place of the firstborn, the first male offspring from every Israelite woman.* [17] *Every firstborn male in Israel, whether human or animal, is mine. When I struck down all the firstborn in Egypt, I set them apart for myself.* [18] *And I have taken the Levites in place of all the firstborn sons in Israel.* [19] *From among all the Israelites, I have given the Levites as gifts to Aaron and his sons to do the work at the tent of meeting on behalf of the Israelites and to make atonement for them so that no plague will strike the Israelites when they go near the sanctuary.*

[20] *Moses, Aaron and the whole Israelite community did with the Levites just as the Lord commanded Moses.* [21] *The Levites purified themselves and washed their clothes. Then Aaron presented them as a wave offering before the Lord and made atonement for them to purify them.* [22] *After that, the Levites came to do their work at the tent of meeting under the supervision of Aaron and his sons. They did with the Levites just as the Lord commanded Moses.*

[23] *The Lord said to Moses,* [24] *"This applies to the Levites: Men twenty-five years old or more shall come to take part in the work at the tent of meeting,*

Levites cannot just enter into the tabernacle and just begin to minister. There should be procedure that is set forth even during the week that prepares them for their assignment. Let's look at how David set procedure for the Levitical Priests.

1 Chronicles 23:[1] *When David was old and full of years, he made his son Solomon king over Israel.*

[2] *"He also gathered together all the leaders of Israel, as well as the priests and Levites.* [3] *The Levites thirty years old or more were counted, and the total number of men was thirty-eight thousand.* [4] *David said, "Of these, twenty-four thousand are to be in charge of the work of the temple of the Lord and six thousand are to be officials and judges.* [5] *Four thousand are to be gatekeepers and four thousand are to praise the Lord with the musical instruments I have provided for that purpose.*

[6] *David separated the Levites into divisions corresponding to the sons of Levi: Gershon, Kohath and Merari."*

Verse [31]*"… The required number of Levites served in the Lord's presence at all times, following all the* <u>procedures</u> *they had been given.*

[32] *And so, under the supervision of the priests, the Levites watched over the Tabernacle and the Temple and faithfully carried out their duties of service at the house of the Lord."*

A modern day S.O.P. should be a document that spells out, with description, procedure and responsibilities of the Levitical Priests at your local ministry. This S.O.P. should include the following topics:

- Attendance
    - absences/tardiness
    - sabbaticals/leave of absences/resignation
    - substitutions

- Attire/Garments

- Compensation (*if there is any*)

- Contracts (*if there are any*)

- Chain of Command* (*see flowchart description on page 186*)

- Guidelines

- Performance Evaluations

- Professional Growth and Development

- Rehearsals/Prep

- Responsibilities

- Repertoire

- Personnel

  o Who are the leaders

  o What are the assignments

To maintain Order, let's look at additional Davidic characteristics that are vital to Order.

Levites were appointed.

1 Chronicles 15:[16] "*David told the leaders of the Levites to appoint their fellow Levites as musicians to make a joyful sound with musical instruments: lyres, harps and cymbals.*"

Notice here that David stated that the Levites are to appoint their fellow Levites. Why is this? Because people from a profession know when those in their profession are legitimate in the skill-set required. A singer can identify another singer, a dancer can identify another dancer, a musician can identify another musician, an intercessor can identify another intercessor, and a servant can identify another servant. It's the same in the natural, a physician can identify another physician, and an attorney can identify another attorney. You know who is legitimate. Verse 17 says,

[17] *"So the Levites appointed Heman son of Joel; from his relatives, Asaph son of Berekiah; and from their relatives the Merarites, Ethan son of Kushaiah;"*

These three men were appointed; they didn't audition. This equates that something was already present in them in order to be appointed to a music leadership position. What we must remember is that you do not audition to be a worship leader…worship is either in you or it is not and if it is in you then you will be identified and set in place from among your family of Levites.

Levites are Identifiable.

1 Chronicles 15:[27] *"Now David was clothed in a robe of fine linen, as were all the Levites who were carrying the ark, and as were the musicians, and Kenaniah, who was in charge of the singing of the choirs. David also wore a linen ephod."*

Levitical Priests should have a dress code that identifies them as they present themselves to God for worship. Levitical Priests cannot wear anything they want to wear and present themselves in any kind of way in the Temple. There is Order in uniformity. Also, the dress code should be identifiable of a Levite not drawing attention to the physical nature of your body but to the spiritual nature of your assignment. How can you effectively carry God's anointing if there is more body showing than garment? Can I see more of you than I can see of Him?

Levites Practice.

1 Chronicles 25:[6] *"All these men were under the supervision of their father for the music of the temple of the Lord, with cymbals, lyres and harps, for the ministry at the house of God. Asaph, Jeduthun and Heman were under the supervision of the king.* [7] *Along with their relatives—all of them trained and skilled in music for the Lord—they numbered 288."*

This passage states, "all of them trained." There should never be an instance where the Levitical Priests just show up at the Temple untrained, unprepared, unlearned. We must present God with our best.

Rehearsals, training, prep, and workshops should be commonplace in keeping Order within the music ministry.

Order keeps the ministry in sequence, arranged and organized. It keeps the ministry from being infiltrated.

> *"Belief and Order give strength. Have to clear rubble before you can build."*
>
> *Robert Jordan, Lord of Chaos*

PERVERSION

"The integrity of the upright shall guide them: but the perverseness of transgressors shall destroy them."

Proverbs 11:3

Perversion is, *"the alteration of something from its original course, meaning, or state to a distortion or corruption of what was first intended"*. The Greek word for perversion is DIASTREPO which means, "opposite from the form it should be (upon creation)."

The first thing you must understand before you read this chapter is that perversion is not limited to nor deals solely with sex. Something can be perverse and not deal with sex at all. We repeatedly hear people speak from the pulpit that "there is a spirit of perversion in this place." Well, what in this place has become perverse? Can you identify what has been taken off its original course from which it was created?

We must remember that perversion is deadly, and it attacks many areas in daily life. When a man has become perverted, he acts like a woman. When a woman becomes perverted, she acts like a man. When a child becomes perverted, they act in rebellion. When marriage becomes perverted, couples live as if they are single. When Government has become perverted, it operates in corruption and unjust policy. When Business & Commerce is perverted, it launders money and operates in unbalanced scales.

Perversion attacks the Levitical Priests as well. When the minstrels become perverted, they only play for money and are not concerned about hearing the frequency of God and amplifying the sound of God in the temple. When the psalmist becomes perverted, they only sing when they are scheduled to lead, or their focus is to become an artist and not to glorify God and exalt His name. When the priest becomes perverted, he is more concerned about his suit than souls and needs to raise his own offering so that he can make sure personal financial benchmarks are met. When the gatekeepers become perverted, they want to be seen praying in the pulpit and not concerned about the spiritual policing of the temple. When the praise team or choir becomes perverted, the focus is an album or how often we are on the schedule and not the assignment of carrying God's anointing.

Levitical Priests must be cognizant that we do not allow the spirit of perversion to come in and take us off our original course and corrupt us from what we were first intended to do. Our original course was that we attach ourselves to God, we are set apart for service, and we carry his anointing. Maintaining Order prevents this. Order keeps you in alignment with your original course. Order keeps the ministry focused on the assignment. Order keeps perversion at bay.

How do we recognize perversion, the biggest spirit of perversion that is attacking the Levitical Priests is whoredom. And within whoredom, there are two areas and those are idolization and promiscuity.

Not only have the Levitical priests become oversexed and desensitized to sex (which we will discuss later in this chapter) and confused about our sexual orientation and lifestyle but we crave to be worshiped. This has not taken place because we are bad people, but one of the reasons this has taken root is because of idolization.

To idolize means to, "*worship as a God.*" We are now worshipping our pastors and first ladies, gospel artists, worship leaders, and musicians. God has been escorted out of his own home and pastors, and their wives have become our gods. And when something becomes a "God", you treat it as such, but also, the "God" expects and demands to be worshiped. We have more armor bearers than the President of the United States has security. We have more processionals than the Queen of England. We spend more time with our leaders than we do our families. We fight for our leaders more than we do our children and spouses. If our leaders are on vacation, we take a vacation from church. Idolization has taken root among the Levites. Yes, the pastor is the angel of the house, but they are not the God of the house. Yes, the worship leader facilitates worship in the house, but they are not to receive it. Your music director may be the best minstrel or producer available in the USA, but they are not to get the glory. What has taken place is we come to church and acknowledge God, but we worship the leaders in position. We must return God back to His residence, His temple, and His sanctuary. We must return to worshiping God and acknowledging the leaders. And the only way this is going to happen is if the Leaders stop demanding it. If we stop demanding that we are worshiped, the laymen won't do it.

The other area in whoredom is promiscuity, and this usually goes hand in hand with idolization. If someone(s) is being idolized, there is usually promiscuity going on as well and if not, it is on its way. The reason promiscuity has infiltrated the Levitical priest is because we have not dealt with the root of the problem. Promiscuity comes from somewhere; it just doesn't appear. It is a fruit birth from a seed that has been planted and not been uprooted and destroyed. Many of our Levitical priests have been sexually abused. Engaged in sexual activity at an early age, been in affairs when we were single with married folk, exposed to pornography and other forms of sexually explicit material and/or we have had intimacy deficiencies in their marriages that in the end when not addressed, lead them astray and into affairs or soliciting prostitutes. We must get to the heart of the matter, the source, deal with the curse, and kill the root/weed.

This root tends to start early. The enemy wants to pollute the mind and the younger he can start corrupting a young mind the better, and the first way it usually starts is via music. One of the prime sources of why our young people act the way they do is because of the music they are listening too. Today's music is infused with sexual lyrics, overtones, and seductions and this music infiltrates the spirit of the person who listens which causes them, in time, to respond. Additionally, a young person can easily and accidentally open a door to promiscuity via the internet that exposes them to the worst pornographic material out there. Once the eyes see it, it enters the mind and opens the door for demonic activity that causes us to act upon it. Or they are experiencing sexual abuse in the home from an adult or seeing sexual abuse among their parents or extended family. And people grow up, and it is never addressed naturally or spiritually, and it manifests itself in the adult age, especially when we get into positions of leadership and authority.

When there are intimacy issues in a marriage where one marriage partner's needs are going unfilled the one that is unfilled can fall under attack/temptation drawing them into sin. 1 Corinthians 7:[5] *"Do not deprive each other except perhaps by mutual consent and for a time, so that you may devote yourselves to prayer. Then come together again so that Satan will not tempt you because of your lack of self-control".* The progression is identifiable, measurable, and predictable and God cared enough about us that He warned us. James 1:[14] *"but each person is tempted when they are dragged away by their own evil desire and enticed.* [15] *Then, after desire has conceived, it gives birth to sin; and sin, when it is full-grown, gives birth to death."* So there is a progression line here…wrong desires, enticement, wrong acts, sin…leads to death. Today we can find sexual opportunities everywhere. The internet has become a new place to solicit evil. (*The Ashley Madison website which was recently hacked in 2015 and leaked names was dedicated to married people looking for affairs had 33 million active accounts.*)

How do we overcome this stronghold? We must:

1. Be sure Jesus is Lord in your life.

Search your heart/life and make sure He is ruling and reigning from the throne of your life. Has He taken control of all of our desires in our hearts, minds or have we truly given Him everything.

2. Tear every idol out of your heart.

If there is anything that you invest more time, talent, and passion in your life, more than you do in your love for God, it's an IDOL...deal with it immediately.

3. Bind the spirits of harlotry and whoredoms that may have taken root in your life.

You must come against this spirit through prayer, and when needed, healing and deliverance need to take place.

"Perversion is a sleeping monster; art is a fanning mistress. Art serves the perversion that is deep and often dormant within human beings."

Thiruman Archunan

THE THREE-HEADED MONSTER

"A worthless person, a wicked man, goes about with crooked speech, winks with his eyes, signals with his feet, points with his finger, with perverted heart devises evil, continually sowing discord; therefore calamity will come upon him suddenly; in a moment he will be broken beyond healing."

Proverbs 6:12-15

There are three spirits that have manifested themselves among the Levitical Priesthood that we must keep an eye out for. They are the spirit of Jezebel, the spirit of Ahab and the spirit of Absalom.

Jezebel

The book of I Kings beginning in chapter 16 tells us about Jezebel, The daughter of Ethbaal, the king of the Zidonians, and the wife of Ahab, the king of Israel. This was the first time that a king of Israel had allied himself by marriage with a heathen princess. She was a great instigator of persecution against the saints of God. Guided by no principle, restrained by no fear of either God or man, passionate in her attachment to her heathen worship, she maintained idolatry around her. 450 prophets ministered under her care to Baal, besides 400 prophets, which ate at her table. The idolatry, too, was of the most debased and sensual kind. Her conduct was in many respects very disastrous to the kingdom both of Israel and Judah. In the end, she came to an untimely death. As Jehu rode into the gates of Jezreel, she looked out at the window of the palace, and said, *"Had Zimri peace, who slew his master?"* He looked up and called to her servants, who instantly threw her from the window, and she was dashed to pieces on the street, and his horses trod her under their feet. She was then consumed by the dogs of the street. Her name came to be used for a wicked woman in Revelation 2:[20], *"Nevertheless, I have this against you: You tolerate that woman Jezebel, who calls herself a prophet. By her teaching she misleads my servants into sexual immorality and the eating of food sacrificed to idols".*

Jones' Dictionary of Old Testament Proper Names has "Jezebel," translated as meaning *"without cohabitation."* This simply means this spirit refuses "to live together" or "cohabit" with anyone. It is divisive to the core and seeks sole proprietorship through manipulation. This spirit will not dwell or exist with anyone else unless they can control the relationship, organization or ministry. It is important to note that this spirit cannot exist without an Ahab in position. This spirit is directly co-dependent on an Ahab. It must have someone in leadership for it to link to or attach itself to so that it can manipulate them. This spirit must be able to link itself with someone of authority so they can begin to coerce policy, procedure and Order. It's also important to note that Jezebel can be a man, it does not have to be a woman, however, many times it is. And the relationship status does not have to be martial. It can be in the form of business, friendship, kinship, but it generally gives off the impression that they are as close as people who are married.

This spirit seems submissive or "servant-like", but it is only for the sake of gaining some strategic advantage. From its core, Jezebel yields to no one.

Jezebel hated the prophets, for the prophets spoke out against her, and she had them killed (1 Kings 18). The prophets were her worst enemies. More than her hatred of the prophets, she hated the Word they spoke from God. Her real enemy was the spoken Word of God. Jezebel had all the prophets killed. What this translates to for us today in the music ministry is that anyone who speaks God's Word, wants to follow His Word, wants to do things His way, wants to bring accountability and protocol or one who will speak up against what this spirit is doing, Jezebel will come against and seek to destroy them.

What we must keep in mind about the spirit of Jezebel is that Jezebel:

1. Wants to be in total control.

    •   Jezebel has an obsessive passion for domineering and controlling others, especially in the spiritual realm. When she became queen, she began a relentless campaign to rid Israel of all evidence of worshipping God. She ordered the extermination of all the prophets of the Lord and replaced their altars with Baal. (1 Kings 18)

• In today's music ministry, anyone who is in leadership or authority and is following God's plan and Order, Jezebel wants them and all remnants of that person destroyed so they can have total control, even if those people and policies are working. Jezebel seeks to establish their policy and people. Jezebel also seeks to distance themselves from the prophets and intercessor of the Temple. There is no collaboration there. Jezebel wants their word, and protocol followed, not Gods. To do this, they **must** have a relationship with the Priest. They must have access and the ear of the Priest.

2. <u>Will destroy by any means to have control.</u>

• 1 Kings 21, Naboth, who refused to sell to Ahab land adjoining the palace, rightly declaring that to sell his inheritance would be against the Lord's command. While Ahab sulked and fumed on his bed, Jezebel taunted and ridiculed him for his weakness, then proceeded to have the innocent Naboth framed and stoned to death. Naboth's sons were also stoned to death, so there would be no heirs, and the land would revert to the possession of the king. Such a determination to have one's way to secure and maintain a position with the Priest, no matter who is destroyed in the process, is a characteristic of the Jezebel spirit.

• In today's music ministry, Jezebel is not concerned about doing what is right, they will do and operate in the wrong to have control. They will move to defamation of character, sabotage and set-ups to destroy a person's influence so they can have complete control of the ministry. This physical killing of

Naboth translates into a social killing in today's time. Spreading gossip or sharing conversations through social media, emails, texts, screenshots, and voice recordings to cause the person to be socially killed which in turn causes them to lose their influence and ability to lead. This creates political and strategic impotence in the person attacked that leads to repositioning, resignation and change in membership in the person they seek to destroy and only strengthens the allegiance of Ahab towards Jezebel.

3. <u>Expert in manipulation.</u>

- In 1 Kings 21, we notice that she manipulated Ahab by emotionally taunting Ahab and then concocted false accusations against Naboth to get him out of the way for possession of the vineyard.

- Jezebel seeks to manipulate Ahab, always having his ear and being able to say things to Ahab to get him to allow Jezebel to act.

- In the modern day music ministry, this person has complete access to the Priest. Has his/her cell phone, house phone, work phone, office hours, can stop by the house, pop up in the office, meet with them directly after service, goes to lunch, dinner and events with the Pastor, the Pastor's spouse even likes this person. When Jezebel calls, Ahab answers. When Jezebel wants a meeting, Ahab clears their schedule. When Jezebel brings accusations, Ahab believes it. When Jezebel wants something done, Ahab makes it happen. When Jezebel wants people out of the way, Ahab removes them.

- Jezebel may also know intimate things about the Priest that they can hold as ransom. Jezebel may know their past, issues, habits that they can use to control the priest if they are ever removed or replaced. They use this knowledge of "intimate things" to manipulate the Priest as needed.

To remove Jezebel, you have to remove Ahab first and all remnants. 1 Kings 22. To ensure Ahab cannot return, he has to be replaced with a Jehu, or a righteous man of legitimate authority, willing to act against Jezebel. Jehu acted by having Jezebel killed. 2 Kings 9:30-37. Jehu acted by having all of the false prophets that followed Baal killed. 2 Kings 10:18-26. The new leader has to be willing to act on the removal of Jezebel.

Let's look at the spirit of Ahab.

Ahab

If Ahab exists, Jezebel is already present and in place. One does not exist without the other. Jezebel is in place and speaking in Ahab's ear. Jezebel attaches itself to Ahab either romantically, politically or socially. Ahab does not have to be a man, but usually is, but Ahab has to be in the highest position of authority, has the final word and no one sits above them unless they appoint and approve a person of such authority who can dictate policy and procedure in the Temple. This is what gives Jezebel their power. Ahab must sit in a high position (with authority).

A characteristic to observe with Ahab is that Ahab avoids confrontation at all costs and will, on occasion, blame himself when others insult or betray him. Ahab never puts Jezebel in her place and never regains his authority that he relinquished. Ahab never replaces, fires, expels or terminates Jezebel. Jezebel's reign always ends with his (Ahab) death, the death of Jezebel either physically or spiritually or a death of the ministry itself. In today's music ministry, Ahab will see Jezebel doing wrong, but will not confront her or address the issue(s).

Ahab is over-merciful. This almost certainly guarantees Jezebel's continued behavior seeing the best in every person and overlooking too much. In today's music ministry, Ahab rarely or never keeps Order and is slow to discipline and address problems and issues in the ministry. Ahab allows people that continually abuse and manipulate protocol to do so uncontested. So you see continued tardiness, poor communication, lack of teamwork, members not adhering to garment/wardrobe protocol, missed rehearsals and overall lack of preparedness consistently by the same people, insubordination, verbal abuse and outright disrespect to leadership. Any excuse they make for their behavior is accepted.

There are some basic characteristics that exist when you see this spirit beginning to manifest itself. They are rooted in passiveness, lack of authority and responsibility.

What we must keep in mind about the spirit of Ahab is that Ahab:

1. Forms the wrong relationships.

    • We must keep this scripture in mind when we are chosen people as God spoke. Deuteronomy 7:[2] *"and when the Lord your God has delivered them over to you and you have defeated them, then you must destroy them totally. Make no treaty with them, and show them no mercy. ³ Do not intermarry with them. Do not give your daughters to their sons or take their daughters for your sons, ⁴ for they will turn your children away from following me to serve other gods, and the Lord's anger will burn against you and will quickly destroy you."*

- 1 Kings 16:³¹ *"He not only considered it trivial to commit the sins of Jeroboam son of Nebat, but he also married Jezebel daughter of Ethbaal king of the Sidonians, and began to serve Baal and worship him."*

- Ahab went against God's will and should have married a woman from the Israelites but instead married a Zidonian daughter of a king which included political considerations. He married for position. Because he formed this relationship (marriage) now, he had someone in his ear that could manipulate him. This happened because he did not take worshipping God seriously. It was of no consequence to Ahab to commit the sins of Jeroboam.

- In today's music ministry, you see Ahab placing someone in position over the ministry based on political, financial, business or social advantage and not Kingdom advantage, you "marry" Jezebel right into power and authority based on what can be gained. So you hire the wrong worship leader because they are a recording artist whose spirit is to manipulate the music ministry for their artistry purposes. Or the Priest will hire someone to run the music ministry because it brings the church more prestige in the social arena. Or the Priest will place someone over the music ministry because this person can advance some of the Pastor's personal goals and initiatives that have nothing to do with the church.

2. Careless and Irresponsible.

   • King Ahab left the things of God to his wife Jezebel, and as a result, she led him into her pagan religion, instead of him leading her to follow the true and living God. He followed after Baal.

   • In today's music ministry, Ahab will let spiritual matters and protocol be left up to Jezebel. You will see things "ruled by committee" frequently or asks the members for their opinion far too repeatedly or defer responsibility to Jezebel when Ahab should be the one making the decision or leading.

3. Easily manipulated.

   • Jezebel manipulated Ahab when Naboth refused to give the vineyard to Ahab by playing on his emotions in his leadership position by saying in 1 Kings 21:[7] *"Is this how you act as king over Israel? Get up and eat! Cheer up. I'll get you the vineyard of Naboth the Jezreelite."* And she went on to manipulate his position (authority) as King beginning in verse [8], *"So she wrote letters in Ahab's name, placed his seal on them, and sent them to the elders and nobles who lived in Naboth's city with him. [9] In those letters she wrote: "Proclaim a day of fasting and seat Naboth in a prominent place among the people. [10] But seat two scoundrels opposite him and have them bring charges that he has cursed both God and the king. Then take him out and stone him to death."*

   • In today's music ministry you will see that when issues arise that emotionally bother the Priest whether legitimate or not, Jezebel will rise up to play off those emotions and in a sinister way, seek to resolve them her way. You will also see the Priest being spoken for...but he is never present to speak for himself. Jezebel will always speak for him and use his name as forgery to get things done that she wants. Jezebel is so good at speaking for him that you can't even tell if it's the Priest's words or hers. Announcements, documents, and presentations will go forth in the Priest's name in his absence.

What you must keep in mind is that Ahab is totally aware of who Jezebel is. Usually, he is married to this person, hired this person, works 40 hours a week with this person or admitted this person into the group/organization. But you might ask yourself, "well if Ahab knows who this person is, why won't Ahab do anything about Jezebel?" The reason is that Ahab thinks Ahab...is someone else. He does not realize that Ahab...is him. The spirit of Ahab clouds whoever possesses it. They think that because they have the highest position, or give the final word on matters that Ahab must be someone else, never realizing that every decision they make is being coerced by Jezebel.

The danger to Ahab is that even though Jezebel has caused great calamity in the ministry since he has formed an alliance with her, Ahab will be the one to die first. (1 Kings 22)

Absalom

The spirit of Absalom is by far the most prevalent spirit today in the Body and most are totally unaware of it.

An Absalom Spirit is rooted in hidden contempt, hidden hatred, and hidden revenge generally towards a specific authority figure, but many times person to person, family to family, and member to member because it manifests itself due to <u>unresolved issues</u>. That hatred is usually kept hidden until a time comes where they can act up it in a vengeful manner.

2 Samuel 13. There is an issue that has arisen in the house of David. Not his kingdom, not the temple, but David's home. His daughter Tamar has been raped by her brother Amnon. Absalom, Tamar's other brother, approaches her and asks, *"Has that Amnon, your brother, been with you"? Absalom told Tamar, "Be quiet for now, my sister; he is your brother. Don't take this thing to heart." And Tamar lived in her brother Absalom's house…".* Absalom hates Amnon for this act, but the Bible says that he NEVER says anything…good or bad about Amnon. In the meantime, David hears about this atrocity and is furious, but he too never says anything to Amnon. However, we go to verse 23, and it starts off with something very interesting, it says, *"Two years later…"*

"Two years later…" Absalom goes to his father's house King David and asks King David and his attendants to venture with him and his sheepherders to the border of Ephraim. King David does not want to attend, for there is no need for him to attend and they will just be in the way. And although Absalom urged him to change his mind, King David would not relent. So Absalom asks him if his brother Amnon can come instead. King David asks why should he attend, but with the urging of Absalom, he relents and allow Amnon and the rest of King David's sons to go. And in verse 28 this takes place:

[28] *"Absalom ordered his men, 'Listen! When Amnon is in high spirits from drinking wine and I say to you, 'Strike Amnon down,' then kill him. Don't be afraid. Haven't I given you this order? Be strong and brave.'* [29] *So Absalom's men did to Amnon what Absalom had ordered.*

Then all the king's sons got up, mounted their mules and fled. [30] *While they were on their way, the report came to David: 'Absalom has struck down all the king's sons; not one of them is left.'* [31] *The king stood up, tore his clothes and lay down on the ground; and all his attendants stood by with their clothes torn."*

Why is this so significant? Because of "Two years later", I asked God, why between verse 22 and 23 was there a two-year gap? And he replied, "Because David did nothing." The issue was not the rape; the issue was not the killing of Amnon. The issue was that David, as the father, never addressed the issue that arose in his home. Absalom was waiting for David to deal with Amnon and comfort Tamar. But he did nothing, so the issue remained unresolved. So as a result, in that two-year period, the anger, resentment, and contempt built up and manifested itself into a conspiracy and murder.

In today's music ministry and in the church itself, many of the issues that have arisen are simply unresolved issues that have festered because they were never addressed weeks, months and even years ago by leadership. As a result, these issues, then manifest themselves to murder the person or the ministry. We have far too many Levitical priests in leadership who are anointed to sing, preach, play, pray and dance, but lack conflict resolution ability not only in the ministry but also in their personal lives. We can't hide behind ministry and neglect our homes.

In today's music ministry, you will see people upset with the leader because they were replaced on a song, didn't get a chance to direct or lead, was disciplined, or they didn't like how a friend was treated. And nothing is ever said or expressed and these feelings will remain dormant and will grow and grow and become unquenchable until they see a way open to act upon it.

When you examine this passage of scripture even further, you will also see that Absalom became enraged about an issue that did not involve him. Yes, any normal human being would be upset if their sibling was attacked. However, Absalom was neither a conspirator, initiator nor culpable for the atrocity that took place.

In today's music ministry, you will see people upset and seek revenge against others concerning issues that did not involve them. Upset about trivial things many of which do not involve the ministry at all.

There are also some additional characteristics that exist when you see this spirit beginning to manifest itself to sabotage the person there is an unresolved issue with. They are rooted in false humility and betrayal.

Here is what we must keep in mind about the spirit of Absalom, Absalom:

1. <u>Seeks an audience.</u>

    • 2 Samuel 15:[2] *"He would get up early and stand by the side of the road leading to the city gate. Whenever anyone came with a complaint to be placed before the king for a decision, Absalom would call out to him, 'What town are you from?' He would answer, 'Your servant is from one of the tribes of Israel.'"*

    • In today's music ministry, this spirit seeks to gain people on its side by building momentum to gain a case against leadership. They realize that there is power in support. So it makes the people believe he is on their side and that their issue is legitimate.

• Similar to what politicians do today. When it is election time, politicians travel all around their jurisdiction, seeking an audience, to hear the people's complaints and they tell everyone that all of their issues are legitimate, and once in office they will address all of their complaints. But the entire point is to disclaim the incumbent, regardless if they are effective or not, to gather votes to be placed in position.

2. A Spirit of Absalom manifests in self-promotion.

• 2 Samuel 15:[3] *"Then Absalom would say to him, 'Look, your claims are valid and proper, but there is no representative of the king to hear you.'* [4] *And Absalom would add, 'If only I were appointed judge in the land! Then everyone who has a complaint or case could come to me and I would see that they receive justice.'"*

• Once this spirit gains support by questioning everyone or picking and prying into everyone who has a complaint, they unify them by making claims that only if they were in charge, there would be no issues or everyone who had a complaint, it would be always settled in their favor. Absalom is a conspirator.

• In today's music ministry, nothing the leadership does is good enough. Even if most of their ideas that are implemented make the ministry better, it will never be good enough. Fault will always be found. They plant doubt concerning leadership. They also find faults in leaders usually not based on anything related to their ability to do the job, and minor things are made major issues, i.e., marital status, attire, financial status, friends, and acquaintances or previous relationships.

3. Kills with kindness.

- 2 Samuel 15:[5] *"Also, whenever anyone approached him to bow down before him, Absalom would reach out his hand, take hold of him and kiss him.* [6] *Absalom behaved in this way toward all the Israelites who came to the king asking for justice, and so <u>he stole the hearts of the people of Israel</u>."*

- In today's music ministry, this spirit steals the hearts of people by being overly attentive. They may suggest meeting over coffee, tea or for "fellowships" at their house to have discussions that are disguised as meeting to hear your concerns but they manifest into discussions and complaints about and against the leader. This is all part of the plan to eventually supplant this person, eventually requesting meetings with their supervisor or the Priest. If the person they are against is the pastor. An Absalom Spirit seeks to eventually "dethrone" and replace the one in authority by planting seeds of discord among the congregation, trustees or board members.

What you must firmly remember about the spirit of Absalom is that the bitterness against authority is specific. Absalom is just not bitter against ANY person in authority, he is bitter about someone specific in authority, and this bitterness is rooted in a personal problem that has gone unresolved. Too many of our Levitical Priests allow the enemy to attach itself to personal issues we have with someone in leadership, and when that happens, that personal problem manifests itself into an eventual coup attempt to overthrow them. Most of the issues that we have with one another could be resolved by a 15-minute discussion at Starbucks over a cup of coffee or a 30-minute discussion over a garden salad at Panera Bread. We shout, prophesy, sing, dance, preach, play, pray while having unresolved issues with one another that manifests itself once that person is put in a position of authority.

You must remember that the spirit of Absalom never manifests when the person is the wrong choice for the ministry only when it is the RIGHT choice. Yes, David mishandled his home, but he was still God's choice, not man's choice. It was deeper than David being Absalom's father in the natural, but in the spirit, it was because David was His choice. Had it been anyone else who was not chosen by God, Absalom more than likely would not have rose up.

Finally, in today's music ministry, Absalom does not want to be disciplined for coming late to rehearsal, for not knowing the material, for not being in proper garments, for not following protocol especially if he got away with it under previous leadership. When Absalom sees that Order will be restored and what was permitted under past leadership will be undone, and they can no longer get away with things of the past, he will rise up.

All these of these spirits mentioned above must be addressed. They can no longer be ignored in the Levitical priesthood. They keep the assignments of the Levitical priesthood from being fulfilled.

"The world will not be destroyed by those who do evil, but by those who watched them without doing anything"

Albert Einstein

SPIRITUAL MAPPING FOR THE MUSIC MINISTRY & INDUSTRY

By Elder Donna Carpenter, Gatekeeper.

Spiritual Mapping can be connected into any sphere of Influence when looking to make an impact and influence. It is an attempt to see an area as it really is and not only as it appears to be. There is as much or more taking place in the realm of the spirit as it is in the natural. This is a discipline of discerning and diagnosis of obstacles to bring revival in a culture through fervent prayer using diligent research and planning.

Cindy Jacobs says," *it is the researching of a city or sphere to discern any inroads Satan has made, which prevent the spread of the gospel and it's evangelization for the Kingdom.*" Victor Lorenzo is an experienced mapper in Argentina. He believes that spiritual mapping combines research, divine revelation and confirmatory evidence in order to provide complete and exact information to be aware of.

Harold Caballeros says that *"what an X-ray is to a physician, spiritual mapping is to intercessors."* Ephesians 6:12 reminds us by saying *"for we are not wrestling with flesh and blood (contending only with physical opponents) but against the despotisms, against the powers against (the masters spirits who are) the world rulers of this present darkness, against forces of wickedness in the heavenly (supernatural sphere)."* This passage of scripture serves notice to believers of the plans of our enemy and how he operates. Each sphere has its assigned and appointed enemies and principalities. As Intercessors and Ministers of Music, we must be skillful using targeted, effective, fervent prayer types and strategies such as Spiritual Mapping to get past the hindrances and blockages.

Spiritual Mapping is what's known as preparation to invade Mountains, Societies, Cultures & Spheres such as Arts and Entertainment related to the Christian Music Ministry & Industry for Kingdom Advancement. Specific Authority is needed to be exercised for taking dominion over enemies. The Hivites listed in Deuteronomy 7:1 are described as nations greater and mightier than we are; this is the spirit that sits atop Arts & Entertainment/ Celebration. The Lord says we are not to be ignorant of Satan's devices, strategies, and methods, but fully aware by scriptures and his spirit. The Hivites occupy and control through counterfeit and perversion to misrepresent the industry. The first Hivite encounter is found in Genesis 34:1-2 in a rape of Dinah by Shechem the son of Hamor the Hivite. Her purity was violated by deception. Pure worship leads us to the presence of the Lord. In his presence is the fullness of Joy.

Spiritual Mapping is not new, in Ephesian 6:18 exhortation to pray ALL types of prayers is encouraged as it states, *"[18] And pray in the Spirit on all occasions with all kinds of prayers and requests. With this in mind, be alert and always keep on praying for all the Lord's people*". To be alert, you must be AWARE, and you must have foreknowledge. You must be able to see ahead in the spirit even before you arrive. This comes through prayer.

Music and the Sounds released through the varying instruments should show forth the creativity of Elohim. This Elohistic name of God represents his covenant of creativity. The Music Ministry & Industry produces and releases sounds that effect and penetrate our spirits. A study of the names of God helps us understand the purposes and character of our God to call upon him appropriately as needed. My prayer is that the Holy Spirit will bring each reader of this book renewed revelation to enter the gates. The music ministry & industry must be aware concerning enemies, principalities, and rulers of darkness that operate. Our mission as Levitical Priest is to establish the Kingdom for our Lord. The mountain of celebration includes various arts, music, movies, sports, fashion, entertainment, and every other way we celebrate and enjoy life. For the majority of the time, it has been possessed, perverted, controlled and ruled by Satanic forces. In this present hour, Holy Spirit wants us as never before to have the creativity and passion of Kingdom people to release Holy Ghost controlled believers. He wants us stirred and activated in our awareness to the importance of Spiritual Mapping. Researching patterns, history, behaviors and areas related to music that informs and alerts us what to expect and how to properly approach prayer types like spiritual warfare, binding and loosing, etc. We must see past pop culture and present what comes from being in the presence of the Lord. Christian music ministries and artists have a supernatural source available to produce the sounds and creativity of Heaven. We should not compromise our worship and give allegiance to other Gods. Idolatry, pride, selfishness, greed, self-promotion, seduction and pretense are tools used against Levites of Sound. Music (vocal, instrumental, or mechanical sounds having rhythm, melody, or harmony) has such a profound effect on our spirit and soul. Scripture lets us see that it was used to drive evil spirits away as well as release peace to calm a troubled soul. John 10:10a reminds us that *"the thief comes but to kill, steal and destroy."* This deceptive spirit of the Hivite loves to operate as a counterfeit and pervert true worship. We're reminded in John 4:24 *"God is a Spirit (a spiritual being), and those who worship him must worship him in spirit and in truth (reality)"*. We too are a spirit, with a soul, living in a body and called to be sanctified wholly (Thessalonians 5:23) Through the realm and the vehicle of the spirit, we can travel to and through places to infiltrate impact, influence and make a difference.

As a map gives direction and helps us reach destinations without delay Spiritual Mapping is a type of Spiritual GPS navigation system application to avoid delays, missed appointments and wandering around losing time, even as the Israelites did 40 years in the wilderness (Numbers 32:13). With all the technology and advancement in these current times, we believers should tap into the prayer application of **SPIRIT**ual **MAP**ping. The significance with gatekeepers/intercessors is to guard as Watchman and assure that all Glory goes to God. The connection to Music Ministry & Industry and Spiritual Mapping is desired escort and to enter the presence of the Lord to gain access to Heaven's sound.

TIPS FOR ORDER

- Assign

  - Everyone in the music ministry must know their assignment before being released for service. This eliminates confusion and promotes organization. Remember, Order is not telling people what to do, it is giving assignments and making sure assignments are being executed.

- Set Protocol

  - Everyone must know what they can and cannot do and what procedures to follow under all circumstances. You must have an (S.O.P).

- Be Consistent

  - Nothing will undermine your leadership and music ministry more than having different sets of rules for different people because you refuse to enforce the protocol set. It shows signs of weakness and favoritism and will begin to allow manipulation to take root. If there are different sets of rules such as paid staff and unpaid staff/volunteers, convey that upfront. Matthew 5:[37] "*Simply let your 'Yes' be 'Yes,' and your 'No,' 'No'; anything beyond this comes from the evil one.*"

- Make a decision

  - Leaders are respected from their subordinates when they are strong in their decision making. Do not lose the respect of those you lead because you are afraid or lack the ability to make a decision. Even if the decision ends up being the wrong one...make one, you can always correct it. Do not leave matters that require your attention left unresolved.

- Follow the chart

  - Everyone under your leadership should know who the leadership team is and what their roles are. There should also be a flowchart that points out the chain of command and who reports to whom. (See page 186)

- Rules of Engagement

  - Rules of Engagement is defined as: "*a directive issued by a military authority specifying the circumstances and limitations under which forces will engage in combat with the enemy.*"

  - Music Ministries are involved in some level of spiritual warfare every time they minister. Make sure your ministry is trained on what to do as certain situations present themselves during worship.

- Prayer

  - Your biggest ally will be the prayer and intercessory ministry. They are your gatekeepers, befriend them. Form an alliance with them. The gatekeepers will be your first line of defense against the enemy and his tactics. The Three-Headed Monster of Jezebel, Ahab and Absalom will be identified when you have people at the gate. Once these spirits have infiltrated the temple, it may be too late.

- Do not release any entity to minister without individual and corporate prayer first.

- Resolve Conflict

  - If you lack the ability to resolve conflict, you are writing your obituary. If conflict resolution is not part of your skill set, form a committee that addresses and resolve conflicts that will arise in the music ministry with you being a deciding vote if needed. I would suggest a 3 or 5 man committee to hear and address all issues that the immediate leader can't address and make sure that 1 of the members is from the prayer and intercessory ministry.

- Resignation

  - Often, we have already decided that we either have had enough due to things not being in order and we can't fix it, we are ready to transition, or our assignment has been completed. But what we seldom do is leave at the right time or the right way. We wait for the next argument, misunderstanding, cut in pay, reorganization or change in leadership, then we get mad and leave storming out the door in a blaze of glory. This is not Order. Don't leave in those moments. If you need to resign, make sure you have stabilized the area you are responsible for. Leave it clean, not messy and leave proper leadership in place if you have a voice in who your replacement will be. Also, in your resignation, include tasks/initiatives completed and accomplishments under or during your tenure and identify what issues that still need to be addressed. Remember, always leave when the waters are calm, not when the waters are troubled.

- ## Resign!

  - Remember, the ball is in your court. If you do not want to follow order and be subject to authority, you can always play the last card in your hand, and that is you can resign.

- ## Control your Spirit

  - Be sure you do not develop a wrong spirit which you can transfer to others. Proverbs 25:28 *"He that hath no rule over his own spirit is like a city that is broken down, and without walls."* When you have a city without walls, anything can leave, but also…anything can enter.

- ## Guard your Tongue

  - The tongue can be used to create a breach in the spirit and provide access to the enemy. Proverbs 15:4 *"A wholesome tongue is a tree of life: but perverseness therein is a breach in the spirit."* Watch what you say and who you say it to. Use your mouth for life, not death.

- ## Select your Associates

  - Proverbs 22:24*"Make no friendship with an angry man; and with a furious man thou shalt not go;* 25*Lest thou learn his ways, and get a snare to thy soul."* Leaders, you must choose your associates wisely. Oftentimes, our friends end up influencing us, not the other way around.

PERSONNEL

"Like an archer who wounds everyone, So is he who hires a fool or who hires those who pass by."

Proverbs 26:10

The single biggest problem in the church today, particularly in music ministry, is that we have put the wrong people in position. A Plan cannot be developed, and Order will not take place if the wrong person has been hired, positioned or placed in leadership. We must stop making our personnel decisions based solely on external factors such as talent, ability, social status, financial stability, etc., when you do that, the person hired rarely provides stability and will contaminate the environment they were entrusted to nurture. Let's examine 1 Samuel on the issue of personnel and see how key this was in the eventual set up of the New Testament music ministry.

1 Samuel 16:[1] *"And the LORD said unto Samuel, 'How long wilt thou mourn for Saul, seeing I have rejected him from reigning over Israel? fill thine horn with oil, and go, I will send thee to Jesse the Bethlehemite:*

for I have provided me a king among his sons'.

² *And Samuel said,' How can I go? if Saul hear it, he will kill me'. And the L*ORD *said, 'Take a heifer with thee, and say, I am come to sacrifice to the L*ORD.

³ *And call Jesse to the sacrifice, and I will shew thee what thou shalt do: and thou shalt anoint unto me him whom I name unto thee.'*

⁴ *And Samuel did that which the L*ORD *spake, and came to Bethlehem. And the elders of the town trembled at his coming, and said, Comest thou peaceably?*

⁵ *And he said, 'Peaceably: I am come to sacrifice unto the L*ORD*: sanctify yourselves, and come with me to the sacrifice.' And he sanctified Jesse and his sons, and called them to the sacrifice.*

⁶ *And it came to pass, when they were come, that he looked on Eliab, and said, 'Surely the L*ORD*'s anointed is before him.'*

⁷ *But the L*ORD *said unto Samuel,' Look not on his countenance, or on the height of his stature; because I have refused him: for the L*ORD *seeth not as man seeth; for man looketh on the outward appearance, but the L*ORD *looketh on the heart.'*

⁸ *Then Jesse called Abinadab, and made him pass before Samuel. And he said, 'Neither hath the L*ORD *chosen this.'*

⁹ *Then Jesse made Shammah to pass by. And he said, 'Neither hath the L*ORD *chosen this.'*

¹⁰ *Again, Jesse made seven of his sons to pass before Samuel. And Samuel said unto Jesse,' The L*ORD *hath not chosen these.'*

¹¹ And Samuel said unto Jesse,' Are here all thy children?' And he said, 'There remaineth yet the youngest, and, behold, he keepeth the sheep.' And Samuel said unto Jesse,' Send and fetch him: for we will not sit down till he come hither.'

¹² And he sent, and brought him in. Now he was ruddy, and withal of a beautiful countenance, and goodly to look to. And the LORD said, 'Arise, anoint him: for this is he.'

¹³ Then Samuel took the horn of oil, and anointed him in the midst of his brethren: and the Spirit of the LORD came upon David from that day forward. So Samuel rose up, and went to Ramah."

There are several key components under personnel just from this passage alone that I want to discuss before we move further along in the Personnel discussion.

<u>Is the person you currently have, the person God wants?</u>

In verse 1, God tells Samuel, *"How long wilt thou mourn for Saul, seeing I have rejected him from reigning over Israel?"* Saul refused to follow the instructions of the judge and priest Samuel by not being obedient. We always mourn over someone that is leaving, left or been replaced, but was that the right person for the job or were they the people's choice?

<u>Do not make your decision on personnel based on appearance and talent alone.</u>

In verse 6, Samuel looked at Eliab and just based off his looks, determined that he must have been the one that God wanted. Many times in music ministry, we hire, place, and position people based solely on the outward appearance. If so, you are making a mistake. You must also look at the person's heart, their purpose and intent must be examined.

The best choice may be the forgotten one.

In verse 11, Samuel had to ask Jessie had all of his sons passed before him. David's own father forgot about him. Sometimes your own family won't even know what's in you and have to be reminded of it. Those that are among you that you sing, play, dance, pray, teach, and minister with won't know what you possess and will have to be reminded that you even exist. When you are making personnel decisions, make sure that you review everyone and eliminate accordingly. Look at your list carefully; there may be someone that you are overlooking that may be the best person for the position who is the least among them.

Once chosen, just because you have been called…it doesn't mean it's your time.

In verse 12, David was chosen and anointed, but in verse 13, after Samuel anointed David, is says that, "*Samuel rose up, and went to Ramah.*" Samuel left, and David returned to keeping the sheep. Why may it not be your time, even though you have been called?

God has to replace Saul first.

You may have been called and anointed for the position, but it is not your time yet because the king that currently reigns needs to be replaced first. God rejected Saul in year 2 of his reign, but it was another 38 years before he was replaced. Two Kings can't reign at the same time on the same throne. Keep in mind that you also may have to serve the person you are replacing for a while before you are placed in position. Let's take a look:

1 Chronicles 16:[14] *"Now the Spirit of the Lord had departed from Saul, and an evil spirit from the Lord tormented him.*

[15] *Saul's attendants said to him, 'See, an evil spirit from God is tormenting you.* [16] *Let our lord command his servants here to search for someone who can play the lyre. He will play when the evil spirit from God comes on you, and you will feel better.'*

[17] *So Saul said to his attendants, 'Find someone who plays well and bring him to me.'*

[18] *One of the servants answered, 'I have seen a son of Jesse of Bethlehem who knows how to play the lyre. He is a brave man and a warrior. He speaks well and is a fine-looking man. And the Lord is with him.'*

[19] *Then Saul sent messengers to Jesse and said, 'Send me your son David, who is with the sheep.'* [20] *So Jesse took a donkey loaded with bread, a skin of wine and a young goat and sent them with his son David to Saul."*

Before you are placed in a position to <u>lead</u>, you may be <u>placed</u> in a position to <u>serve</u> the person you will replace. Do not despise this because there are many things you can learn that will be vital to your success once in authority. Also, this will teach you to still serve those that rise against you. Persecution is part of the process. (Before David was King, Saul tried to kill him), 1 Samuel 19.

However, this can backfire on you. Even though you are the right choice and have been placed in leadership, you still have to make the correct personnel decisions once you are in your position. Let's take a look at what happens when you make the wrong personnel decisions.

1 Chronicles 13:[1] *"David conferred with each of his officers, the commanders of thousands and commanders of hundreds.*

[2] He then said to the whole assembly of Israel, 'If it seems good to you and if it is the will of the Lord our God, let us send word far and wide to the rest of our people throughout the territories of Israel, and also to the priests and Levites who are with them in their towns and pasturelands, to come and join us.

[3] Let us bring the ark of our God back to us, for we did not inquire of it during the reign of Saul.'

[4] The whole assembly agreed to do this, because it seemed right to all the people.

[5] So David assembled all Israel, from the Shihor River in Egypt to Lebo Hamath, to bring the ark of God from Kiriath Jearim.

[6] David and all Israel went to Baalah of Judah (Kiriath Jearim) to bring up from there the ark of God the Lord, who is enthroned between the cherubim—the ark that is called by the Name.

[7] They moved the ark of God from Abinadab's house on a new cart, with Uzzah and Ahio guiding it.

[8] David and all the Israelites were celebrating with all their might before God, with songs and with harps, lyres, timbrels, cymbals and trumpets.

[9] When they came to the threshing floor of Kidon, Uzzah reached out his hand to steady the ark, because the oxen stumbled. [10] The Lord's anger burned against Uzzah, and he struck him down because he had put his

hand on the ark. So he died there before God."

There were some key mistakes David made in this passage of scripture. Let's take a look.

What's the purpose of the Meeting?

In verse 1 in states that David consulted with the captains and with every leader. Be careful of what is on the agenda at the meeting. The agenda for this meeting was to relocate the ark, however, God did not speak to David to make this move of relocating His anointing and presence. When you have meetings with the music ministry, it may seem trivial, but make sure you run the meeting by God first. The agenda for the meeting may be a good idea, but not the correct one for the time.

Don't rule by committee.

The second issue we notice is found in verse 2 when David asked the congregation for their opinion on moving the ark. What you must understand is that every decision cannot go for vote or approval by the people. Here, the people agreed. I'm sure they thought it was a great idea; they thought they would be doing the will of God and above all, they wanted to obey their leader David. But all that seems right, may not be.

Follow Protocol.

As you go down to verse 7, David chooses the personnel to carry the ark. But before we get to that, we notice something very interesting. David did not follow protocol. The specific instructions for carrying the ark was that it was to be carried on poles on the shoulders of 4 Levites as prescribe under Moses. However, in verse

7, we see that the ark was moved on a cart driven by an ox. David did not follow the protocol.

Who is in position?

In verse 7, it names who David put in position to guide the cart. Their names were Uzzah and Ahio. After further study of who Uzzah was, I found that he was not a Levite at all, he was from the Tribe of Benjamin. David had the wrong person in position, and this person was killed. Uzzah should have never been there in the first place.

David should have never placed Uzzah in position to be close enough to the ark to touch it because he was not designated to carry the ark; he was not a Levite. How is this significant for the music ministry? When you put the wrong personnel in place to handle God's anointing in key positions such as minstrels, worship leaders, ministers of music, ministers and elders, they can literally destroy and kill the lives of the people who they are ministering to.

When you have the wrong people handling worship, marriages are not mended, addictions are not overcome, deliverance does not take place, peace does not abound, confusion runs rampant, and perversion begins to take root. Death and destruction take place in the Temple.

I also looked into the meaning of the names of these two individuals who had been placed by the ark. Uzzah and Ahio. Uzzah means "friendly." We have a lot of friendly people in position. They are always politically correct, never wants to rub anyone the wrong way, rarely, if ever, speaks up when things are wrong and always "goes with the flow," never wanting to make waves. This is exactly the wrong person you want in leadership. These types of individuals rarely seek or maintain Order for they want to remain popular with the people.

Ahio means "strong." These individuals can carry the load. People you can count on, they can help out financially more than others, are strong tithers, they have endurance in the ministry for they have been there a long time and weathered the storm of transition. But they are not Levites either. They are simply in position because they can carry it, but they are not anointed for it.

Another key component in this passage of scripture is where were the Levites to speak up? No one said a thing. Not to rebuke David the King, but to provoke him to repent. And get him to see that what he had instructed was not correct. To repent means, "to change one's mind" as God did in Exodus 32 when His anger rose up against the children of Israel and Moses confronted God and in verse 14 it says, *"And the LORD repented of the evil which he thought to do unto his people."* What we forget is that God repented because Moses spoke up. Moses, a Levite said, STOP!! He said something that he knew would go against what God previously proclaimed. In this passage with David, there is not one verse that speaks to any of the leaders of the Levites speaking to David to get him to repent after the decision had been made to move the ark nor to the selection of the personnel. As Levites, you cannot make the Priest act, but you can be a voice when things are heading out of order. The carrying of the ark in this manner was out of order and thus got someone killed. The Levites should have spoken to the King, even if that meant being put to death because God's Order was not being followed.

As Levites, we must remember that we must remain a voice for God's Order. We cannot remain silent and watch the lives of people destroyed for the sake of emotions, position, power, and influence. Lives are literally at stake.

The music ministry must be a place of Order so that God's anointing has "free flow" to move as it needs to.

WHEN YOU DON'T FOLLOW THE PLAN, YOU GET OUT OF ORDER, AND YOU POSITION THE WRONG PEOPLE, WHICH GET'S PEOPLE KILLED.

The other key piece that we want to examine under personnel is identifying Leaders. The first thing you must remember is that the burden of the music ministry is too vast for you to handle it alone. You will wear yourself out; your life will become unbalanced, and your health and family will suffer, and you will fall out of order. You need a team; you need help, and you need assistance. And not only do you need assistance, but you also need the right assistance. Let's take a look. Jethro visits Moses.

Numbers 18:[13] *"The next day Moses took his seat to serve as judge for the people, and they stood around him from morning till evening.*

[14] *When his father-in-law saw all that Moses was doing for the people, he said, 'What is this you are doing for the people? Why do you alone sit as judge, while all these people stand around you from morning till evening?'*

[15] *Moses answered him, 'Because the people come to me to seek God's will.* [16] *Whenever they have a dispute, it is brought to me, and I decide between the parties and inform them of God's decrees and instructions.'*

¹⁷ Moses' father-in-law replied, 'What you are doing is not good.

¹⁸ You and these people who come to you will only wear yourselves out. The work is too heavy for you; you cannot handle it alone.

¹⁹ Listen now to me and I will give you some advice, and may God be with you. You must be the people's representative before God and bring their disputes to him.

²⁰ Teach them his decrees and instructions, and show them the way they are to live and how they are to behave.

²¹ But select capable men from all the people—men who fear God, trustworthy men who hate dishonest gain—and appoint them as officials over thousands, hundreds, fifties and tens.

²² Have them serve as judges for the people at all times, but have them bring every difficult case to you; the simple cases they can decide themselves. That will make your load lighter, because they will share it with you.

²³ If you do this and God so commands, you will be able to stand the strain, and all these people will go home satisfied.'"

Here Jethro, the father-in-law of Moses, pays a visit to him, but when he sees him, he notices that Moses is working day and night on the needs of the people. In doing so, Moses is suffering or soon will begin to experience suffering because he is spending all his time among the people.

What this equates to in today's music ministry is that we have put "church work" above our family and personal well-being and by doing so, our lives have become unbalanced. The choir is not supposed to be more important that your spouse, the praise team is not supposed to be more important than your children; the meeting can wait if your health and sanity are being compromised. You need <u>balance</u>. A Levite is of no use in the infirmary or dead. The proper order is God, Family, Church work: your personal relationship with God, then your relationship with your family and **THEN** the work of the church. If this is not the order, then your life is out of order, and you are what Proverbs 11:1 says is a False Balance or an unbalanced scale.

God does not want us as Levites to be weary in our work. And one of the ways to help us stay in order is that we must select help, and they must possess four qualities. Jethro points out the four qualities that these men must have:

<u>Men of Ability: Able Men.</u>

Do not select people who do not know what they are doing. Make sure they have the skill-set and knowledge to carry out the assignment given.

<u>Men of Godliness: Such as fear God.</u>

Do not select people who will not operate in the fear of God so that God's wrath does not follow. Those who do not fear God, will not obey Him.

<u>Men of God's Word: Men of Truth</u>

Do not select people who do not know God's Word, they can't come from a place of truth when it is time to give Godly counsel or direction.

Men of Honor: Hating Covetousness

Do not select men who will yearn or desire power, positions, and titles. They will manipulate and run schemes.

I once read an email from a person who was over the music ministry at a particular church who was looking for leaders and stated that they did not need to have leadership skills in them. I could have screamed because I said to myself, this is one of the reasons why this music ministry is dysfunctional in the first place, and this is not biblical. And what it shows is that you don't want people who can help, you want people you can control. Let's take a look at what God says about leadership skills.

Numbers 11:[16] "*The Lord said to Moses: 'Bring me seventy of Israel's elders who are known to you as leaders and officials among the people. Have them come to the tent of meeting, that they may stand there with you.* [17] *I will come down and speak with you there, and I will take some of the power of the Spirit that is on you and put it on them. They will share the burden of the people with you so that you will not have to carry it alone.'*"

Moses had the burden of feeding the people, and the people began to complain. Moses was overwhelmed with the responsibility of this so, in verse 16, God clearly states that I will give you help, but there are two requirements in choosing personnel before this help is given.

1. Elders who are known to you as leaders.

God specifically tells Moses to select people who already have a leadership skill set in them. Why would you select a person to lead people who have never managed administrated or supervised people?

I have a buddy of mines who always tells me, "Mike, you can't give what you ain't got." And he is correct. Too many times we ask people to produce fruit from a seed that does not exist and then questions the results when that fruit is not produced. When you need leaders, Only select people who have a leadership skill-set in them and then take what is in YOU and put it in them to make up the difference if it is needed. How do you make up this difference? Through impartation. Not only by the laying on of hands, but by mentoring, training, professional development, reflection, and one-on-one sessions, etc., can leadership skills sets be enhanced.

2. Elders who are known to you as officials among the people.

God states to select people who, are known as officials among the people. What does this mean? Officials in this passage mean to select people who are respected among the people that they will lead. Have you ever worked at a job where the employees did not respect the supervisor? Even if that supervisor had knowledge of the area they supervised. What happens is un-productivity, insubordination and lack of institutional and organizational discipline. If the person you select is not respected, then the people following will not listen to them, and this will affect the productivity of your music ministry. The psalmists will not follow the worship leader if they do not respect them; the minstrels will not follow the music director if they do not respect them and so on. People will follow if they have been ordered to by the Priest, but the lack of respect will damage chemistry and limit the ability of the music department to fulfill its assignment.

This is true even in the natural on January 23rd, 2016, David Blatt, coach of the Cleveland Cavaliers was fired with the best record in the Eastern Conference. Many rumors began to swirl around as to why and who was behind this and the Cleveland Cavaliers' administration began to engage in spin doctoring to keep the public off balance to the reasons why. But it was very clear to me as to what happened. David Blatt was not considered an official among the people he was leading. He was simply not respected by his players, rendering him ineffective and he had to go.

Numbers 27:18 *"So the Lord said to Moses, "Take Joshua son of Nun, a man in whom is the spirit of leadership, and lay your hand on him. 19 Have him stand before Eleazar the priest and the entire assembly and commission him in their presence. 20 Give him some of your authority so the whole Israelite community will obey him."*

I love this above mentioned scripture. Again, God instructs Moses on his successor, and He gives him specific instructions. Not only does God tell him who it is but he states that this man *"in whom is the spirit of leadership."* Joshua already possessed the skill set of a leader. But notice what else he stated, bring him before the priest and the entire assembly and *"commission him in their presence. Give him some of your authority so the whole Israelite community will obey him"*.

What does this look like in today's music ministry? Too many of you have accepted positions where the Priest has not commissioned or established or presented you in front of the assembly and because of this, the people you are responsible for do not obey you. Never and I mean never accept a position of leadership in the music ministry, and the pastor will not commission or establish you. The enemy will notice this and anything that you do that they do not agree with they will circumvent your authority and go directly to the pastor. Many of the issues you may be facing is because you have not been established before the congregation. Even when you start a new position at a company in the natural world, your boss takes you around and introduces you to other staff and lets them know what your position and responsibilities are. Never are you hired and your supervisor doesn't acknowledge that you are part of the team. If the supervisor doesn't acknowledge your position, then the coworkers do not have to acknowledge you either. Don't allow it to happen to you in the Temple. If the pastor won't back you, then you are in for a difficult journey.

"We could probably win more often if we were willing to deploy seasoned personnel and equip them with sufficient carrots and sticks."

Thomas M. Franck

POSITIONS

"You will not have to fight this battle. Take up your posi-tions; stand firm and see the deliverance the LORD will give you, Judah and Jerusalem. Do not be afraid; do not be dis-couraged. Go out to face them tomorrow, and the LORD will be with you."

2 Chronicles 20:17

Assignments cannot be completed, and Order won't be achieved without having personnel in their proper positions. As you saw in the previous chapter, in 1 Chronicles 13, Uzzah was not only the wrong person, but he was in the wrong position as well. He should never have even been close enough to the Ark to touch it.

There is nothing that creates more chaos in ministry than having personnel in the wrong position. Even in the natural, NBA, NFL, NHL and MLB coaches', strategize on positioning and spacing. Not only making sure that each player is in the right position (title), but also in the right location (space) on the field or court to make sure plays can be executed effectively. The Triangle Offense under coach Phil Jackson when he coached the Chicago Bull and

LA Lakers focused on spacing and making sure the player was in the right position. This is why his teams offensive efficiency always rank high. Because he made sure his players were always in the right position on the court.

Before the Temple was built, David received instructions from the Lord and showed Solomon how to divide the priests and the Levites and how they were to serve. (You can review page 186, Music Ministry Flowchart). In the Temple, there were several classes or positions of Levites. The music ministry should have positions that correlate to the time of David. Below is a list of those personnel positions, what they were called under David, what they equate to in the modern day and a corresponding scripture.

Temple of David	Modern Position	Scripture
Priests	Pastors/Overseers	(1 Chronicles 24:1-19)
Priests' Assistants	Elders/Ministers/Etc.,	(1 Chronicles 23:4,28)
Singers	Worship Leader/Psalmists/Choirs	(1 Chronicles 25:7-31)
Musicians	Minstrels	(1 Chronicles 23:5)
Gatekeepers	Intercessors	(1 Chronicles 26:1-19)
Keepers of the Treasure	Trustees/Administration	(1 Chronicles 26:20-28)
*Dance	Dancers	(2 Samuel 6:14 and 1 Chronicles 15:29)

*Dancing was part of the David Worship and we will explore this in later chapters.

"My serve can get better, for sure. It's not about serving bombs, but positioning, variation in speed and spin."

Rafael Nadal

FORGET ABOUT IT

"Brothers, I do not consider that I have made it my own.
But one thing I do: forgetting what lies behind and straining
forward to what lies ahead, I press on toward the goal for
the prize of the upward call of God in Christ Jesus. Let those
of us who are mature think this way, and if in anything you
think otherwise, God will reveal that also to you."

Philippians 3:13-15

Coming up as a kid, I used to collect trading cards. I collected football, basketball, and baseball. My first love as a child was football. Oh, how I remember watching Walter Payton, Tony Dorsett, and Billy Simms run the football and I had plenty of their cards as well as their teammates cards.

I remember laying all of my cards out on the carpet and coming up with teams and trading players among the teams. To me, it was just fun looking on the back of the cards at the player's stats and deciding what player would be better suited for various teams.

I didn't realize at the time that I was operating in the office of a General Manager. I was making personnel decisions with my trading cards.

Once I got older, to this day, I love to watch the NFL and NBA Drafts. I put the dates on my calendar and make sure I have no rehearsals, meetings or events so that I can watch who, where, and why a player is drafted to a particular team. I play the role of General Manager from my couch.

In football, the most important position is the quarterback. Not only are they the highest paid, but they are considered the leaders of the team. Many General Managers have stated that if you don't have a good quarterback, you don't have a good team. But there is something very interesting that I noticed many coaches and general managers say about the quarterback position. They grade this quality higher than physical ability, preparation, upbringing and even the criminal background of the potential prospect. This quality is…does this quarterback has the ability to Forget.

When they bring in potential quarterbacks to be interviewed before the draft, they try to determine does this quarterback have the ability to forget. The teams review film with the player where they made a mistake and question them on how they felt after the mistake. They also review stats following a mistake to see how they performed. They review body language and mood with their teammates after an error was made. Why? Because they have determined that there is a direct correction between success and forgetting. The quarterback and his teammates will make mistakes but can the quarterback get over it so that he can move on to the next play and lead the team to victory.

Can the quarterback forget that he threw an interception on the last play so he can throw a touchdown on the next? Can the quarterback forget that the wide receiver dropped a perfect pass that was in his hands on the last play so that he can throw to him once again when he is wide open on the next play? Can the quarterback forget that his offensive line blew coverage and allowed him to get sacked three times in a row on a series of downs so that on the next series, he can be comfortable in the pocket and make the right pass?

The world teaches us to forgive, but not forget, but what is the benefit to remembering the failures of yourself and others? What success does that bring to the team, music ministry or the church?

A great leader is one that can forgive quickly but forget even quicker. Continuing to remember always keeps you looking back. Continuing to remember keeps a thorn in your flesh that the enemy can prick and pull on to manipulate your emotions. Continuing to remember can be a blind spot in seeing the true gifts and heart of the persons that you lead in your music ministry. Hindering yourself is one thing, but hindering others is quite another because you can truncate the effectiveness of the Temple and Kingdom of God by always remembering the mistakes and issues of the past.

Not only does this hinder your interactions with others, but also with yourself. You may have practiced and worked hard all week on your assignment and get in the service and make a mistake, miss a cue, a dance step or forget a chord change or lyric. But you can't let that affect you for the next time, you can't linger in that. You have to forget because the assignment is far too great for you to linger in an error.

In making personnel decisions, try and select people who have the ability to get over things quickly and who can move on from situations that brought difficulty or where they may have failed. People who continue to remember will hold the ministry back. They will always bring up the past, linger in hurts, continue to circulate issues and tend to have difficulty in getting delivered. People who can never forget, also tend to be people who have difficulty in fostering and developing relationships which hurts the expansion of the music ministry.

There is a word that has frequently been used on the east coast, particularly by the Mafia types and has been carved into our vernacular due to its popularity in the films over the years as the Godfather trilogy and Good Fellas. This word now has made the urban dictionary, this word is, fuhgeddaboutit, which means to literally Forget about it - the issue is not worth the time, energy, mental effort, or emotional resources.

"To be able to forget means sanity."

Jack London

TIPS FOR PERSONNEL

- <u>Know your skill-set AND that of your team</u>

If your talent is not up to par, then you need to make up the difference in other areas. You can't be pointless (talent) AND worthless (value). You may not be the best dancer, musician, singer or preacher in the church...that's ok. But make sure you add value, so it is worth keeping you around. Especially when the church or entity needs to make personnel decisions. Here's what you can do:

- o don't be anti-social (don't be a loner)
- o do not cause discord
- o show up on time for rehearsal (be the first to arrive and last to leave)
- o be an intercessor
- o learn the material (directors know when you have studied the material or not)
- o help set-up equipment (having the band as your ally is powerful)
- o ask, "how can I serve?"

- <u>Refrain from Vain Glory</u>

Talent is a dime a dozen…don't over-rate yourself. There are countless others that are just as talented as you. What makes you different than them? What can you do:

- limit comments, emails, posts, statuses and videos on social media exalting your ability
- incorporate others into the worship service and leadership
- talk about "US" instead of "I"

- ## You are not the only one Anointed

God has His Hand on others not just you. Never cause yourself to feel like if you don't sing, dance, play, pray or preach that God won't move. What can you do:

- rely on others whose talent is more seasoned than yours
- never design or build the music ministry to only succeed if you are present at service, rehearsals, events, etc.
- create an atmosphere for God to move when you are not ministering
- don't suppress those that are anointed, give them an opportunity to minister
- support and encourage others

- ## Take a Stand/Make a Decision

At some point (leaders), you must have enough of a conscience to speak up and stand on what you feel is right, but never lose your influence in doing so…it's called political savvy. Those that you lead lose respect for you when you are fickle in your decision making, especially when it is a matter of right or wrong. Don't say one thing in front of the group and another in front of the Pastor or in private. You undermine your authority. What can you do:

- o make a decision when one needs to be made and don't hesitate
- o stick to the rules, limit exceptions unless absolutely necessary and for valid reasons
- o understand that there is a difference between being **Right** and being **Fair**. Always seek to be Right. Seeking to be Fair tend to cause you to become Politically Correct

- <u>Be utilized…don't be used.</u>

There is a difference between your gift being used and YOU being used because there is no one else or the person desired, is not available. Know where you stand with the leadership and accept it. What can you do:

- o have regular meetings with your leader and pastor
- o find out what leadership wants then determine if you fit into that plan

- <u>Remain Humble</u>

No matter how many times your name is called, or you are patted on the back, stay humble, stay focused.

2 Chronicles 12:[12] *"And when he humbled himself the wrath of the LORD turned from him, so as not to make a complete destruction. Moreover, conditions were good in Judah."*

You want the environment/atmosphere of the music ministry to remain good. Proverbs 16:[18] *"Pride goes before destruction, a haughty spirit before a fall."* To avoid a fall, humility must be present. Make sure you and your team remain humble before the Lord.

- ## Avoid Conflicts of Interest

Do not create a conflict of interest by having the same persons/people occupy multiple positions that overlap, this can lead to ethical problems and indecision. When you create conflicts of interests, you can eliminate a leader's ability to do what is right. Do not create or put yourself in a position to where you have one foot in ministry and the other foot in money. When you pull on one string, three others are pulled. When you speak up on one issue, you expose another issue. When you put one person in position, you eliminate two other positions that you need. Conflict of interest can particularly get sticky when you have married couples occupying several positions in the music ministry or music-related positions.

When I accepted the position in music ministry in 2010, I specifically told Mesha that I would not place her in a significant leadership position because I did not want to create a conflict of interest that could hinder the music ministry when decisions had to be made. Also, I did not want church work to spill over at home and cause issues in the family due to disagreements over music ministry policy and protocol.

The enemy has infiltrated marriages because many Levitical priests are in positions that create conflict. Even in the book of 1 Chronicles, when David began to assign positions, they were all Levites, but they came from different families among the Levites. 1 Chronicles 25

"David and the temple officials chose the descendants of Asaph, Heman, and Jeduthun to be in charge of music. They were to praise the Lord by playing cymbals, harps and other stringed instruments. Here is a list of the musicians and their duties:" Here you see David assigning positions to a variety of families among the Levites, never at any time did one family have all the responsibility.

- <u>Know when you need to change</u>

"There's a different person to lead a business at different stages of development and the Warriors have gone from a "startup" company to an organization looking to maximize its output" Joseph S. Labob-majority owner of the Golden State Warriors commenting on the firing of Coach Mark Jackson.

The firing of Mark Jackson in 2014 was very controversial. Jackson was immensely popular in the Warriors' locker room and was coming off a season in which he won 51 games and got his team within a whisker of upending the third-seeded Clippers, but somehow the ownership felt that there was time for a change at this stage of development in the organization. (The Warriors went on to hire a 1st year coach in Steve Kerr, and they won the championship in his first season). Sometimes who you have in position can only take you so far and then you have to replace them with someone else for the next stage. You must know when this time comes and be ready to make the decision for the betterment of the ministry.

TIPS FOR MUSIC MINISTRY LEADERS

- __Be THE choice...not A choice.__

I graduated from Northern Illinois University in 1994 with a B.A. in Sociology. Before college, I prayed that I wanted to have two full-time jobs. One in music and one in education and God granted me that request. I have worked at four major colleges or universities and before I accepted each position, I always asked the committee chair, "am I who you want...am I your first choice"? If they said no, I did not take the position. Because I knew I would come in with my hands tied, with a blemish, a defect that they perceived or invented that would possibly hinder me from accomplishing the goals of the institution.

On Wednesday, May 7th, 2014, I received a text from Donald Alford II (One of the greatest bass players in Chicago history) to play two songs on his next record. I was honored and humbled by this. But I asked him why did he want me to play, and he said, "I don't want anyone else to cut these two tunes." Immediately something came to me: Be chosen because you are WANTED, not because the other choice is not available. The difficulties you are experiencing in your music ministry may be because you were never the choice of the Pastor in the first place. You can't serve someone who does not want you. However, you can work for them. What can you do:

Ask them upon being offered the position… "Am I your Choice"? As stated in the previous chapter, there was no biblical reference made to an objection from Aaron, the priest, to Moses, when he presented the Levites to him to serve in the tabernacle nor when God chose Joshua was there any objection from Moses.

"In middle school, I got picked on a lot. But boy, it sure felt good to get picked, because who doesn't like to get chosen and called out as special?" - Jarod Kintz

- Keep your team Covered.

Tuesday, May 6th, 2014, I was asked to play drums with the praise team at Pastor Phil Tarver's church, United Faith Center in Blue Island, Illinois. There was a mighty prophetic movement that came through the minstrels. Warfare took place, and a Word came to Pastor Phil Tarver at the end of the flow to lay hands on every person in the room for Peace and Covering.

I'm so glad he prayed for covering because we need it. The enemy wants to destroy those that are responsible for carrying God's anointing, and he wants to exploit their faults, issues, habits to tarnish the Kingdom.

Leaders pray continuously so that the Levitical priests are not devoured and left exposed so that they do not lose their effectiveness and tarnish the Kingdom.

"Tend to the people, and they will tend to the business."– John Maxwell

- <u>Demand a support staff.</u>

The music ministry, in most churches, is the largest ministry in the church by far. This cannot be run by one person alone. Depending on the size of the church, not only do you need to have an assistant but also a staff. If the church cannot afford to put someone on staff, seek volunteer help internally from the music department or church membership. Do not allow your ego to cause you to run it alone. You will soon find yourself overwhelmed and schedules, meeting requests, emails will not be returned.

"No man will make a great leader who wants to do it all himself, or to get all the credit for doing it." – Andrew Carnegie

- <u>Managing is just as important as Music</u>

If you have never held a position where you've had to manage/supervise, this is not the leadership position for you. Yes, you must know music, but you must know how to supervise. Managing people is just as important as knowing chords, scales, songs, teaching, directing, singing and dancing. I have seen great anointed singers get fired because they do not know how to manage. If this is you, get an assistant worship leader, asst. minister of music, asst. choir director, etc., who can cover your deficiencies. Do not leave yourself exposed. In the natural world, business leaders always hire people who can do the job they can't and let them do it.

"Employers are like horses — they require management." – P.G. Wodehouse

- <u>Get a Mentor</u>

We all need someone who we can bounce ideas off of and have someone who knows more than us so they can impart into it. But you also need someone who can hold you accountable.

- Don't lose the anointing. Hopefully, you have it

Spiritually, your greatest asset is the anointing, not your skill-set. Do all you can to not lose God's presence. Because once that happens, you are no longer effective.

- Don't lose the respect of those you lead

Naturally, one of your greatest assets is respect. If the people you lead, lose respect for you, you have all but lost your ability to lead them. They will only follow you because they have to, not because they want to. Remember,

"The key to successful leadership today is influence, not authority."– Ken Blanchard

- Keep skill-set high

Proverbs 22:[29] *"Do you see someone skilled in their work? They will serve before kings; they will not serve before officials of low rank."*

Always select your team from the best people from the highest skill-set. People that are great at what they do have options, don't let great people (those that are skilled in their work) escape, not be selected or be ran away by current members. People that have high skill-sets as minstrels, psalmists, dancers, managers, etc., always want to be around others that are great at what they. They realize that their assignment will be just that much easier to accomplish.

- Encourage

1 Thessalonians 5:[11]*"Therefore encourage one another and build one another up...".* Find someone who wants to build encouragement into a critique. It's not what you say, but often how you say it. When someone knows you believe in them, they will always give you their best. Those that you lead, when you see them doing something good or well, let them know. They will be more apt to repeat that behavior. Always remember that people want to be in great environments. There is no better way to create a positive environment by building in encouragement. Ephesians 4:[29] *"Do not let any unwholesome talk come out of your mouths, but only what is helpful for building others up according to their needs, that it may be benefit those who listen."*

"Outstanding leaders go out of their way to boost the self-esteem of their personnel. If people believe in themselves, it's amazing what they can accomplish." – Sam Walton

- ## Avoid Peter!

In 1969, a book was written by Laurence J. Peter called, "The Peter Principle: Why Things Always Go Wrong." The Peter Principle is a concept in management theory in which the selection of a candidate for a position is based on the candidate's performance in their **current** role rather than on abilities relevant to the **intended** role. Thus, employees only stop being promoted once they can no longer perform effectively and managers rise to the level of their incompetence. Only promote people who can do the intended job, not those who can do their current job well. Just because someone can sing, it doesn't mean they should be the worship leader. Just because someone can play, it doesn't mean that should be the music director. Ability does not equate to leadership skills nor the ability to perform the next task. Avoid Peter!

- ## Don't Cover Up!

Never "add-on" to "cover-up". If you made a mistake in personnel, never add-on new people to cover-up the bad. This never works because those you bring in will eventually become contaminated or they will leave. Clear out the problems BEFORE you bring in new people. Remember, doctors clean out the wound/infection before they bandage it.

- ## Address the 10

We always talk about Joshua and Caleb and we should because they believed that the children of Israel could conquer Canaan. But we always forget about the 10. Moses sent 12 spies to survey Canaan, but 10 of those spies came back with a bad report, and they caused discord among the people, (Numbers 13). These 10 caused hundreds of thousands of people to miss the promise land. 10 caused a generation to miss out on its promise! Leaders, you must address those that are causing the ministry to miss its promise by sowing seeds of discord. Do not allow people who cause discord and division to continue in the music ministry. Any scouts that you send out to survey territory debrief them before they are allowed to go before the people and contaminate them. If anything they say is not in line with the plan, Address them!

- ## Keep the Priest Happy

HEBREWS 13:[17] *"Obey your leaders and submit to them, for they keep watch over your souls as those who will give an account. Let them do this with joy and not with grief, for this would be unprofitable for you"*.

You gain no advantage by being in conflict with your pastor. Make sure that one of your goals is to submit and obey them. Your way will be hard in your position if you are in constant conflict with your pastor. Let them have joy in your work and what you bring to the ministry. It will work in your favor. The music ministry leaders that I have known to have the most success were those who were not in conflict with their pastor.

"The challenge of leadership is to be strong, but not rude; be kind, but not weak; be bold, but not bully; be thoughtful, but not lazy; be humble, but not timid; be proud, but not arrogant; have humor, but without folly." – Jim Rohn

SERVICE

"Let your light so shine before men, that they may see your good works, and glorify your Father which is in heaven."

Matthew 5:16

Many Christians do not believe that the Bible speaks on perception, but it most certainly does. One of the best ways that we can serve God is by being conscious of what we present to the world. What do people see? Do they see Christ in you? As we say so well in the church, "Does your walk match your talk"? But is this something that we are concerned about as Christians? One of the worst phrases we have come up with in the church in this time is, "I don't care what people think about me!" This is by far, in my mind, one of the most idiotic things that we can say as Christians. If this is the Body's thinking, then how can we effectively win anyone to Christ?

I want to take you down a different path than what you would normally think concerning Service. We have many books on how and what is required to be a psalmist, minstrel, intercessor, priest, and dancer. Teachings and workshops have been done all over the country. But let's talk about your perception or,

What Is Your Brand?

Your brand is your promise to your audience. It tells them what they can expect from your products and performance, and it differentiates your offering from your artists and other music ministries. Your brand is derived from who you are, who you want to be and who people perceive you to be. Your sound, Your look, Your reputation and even the company you keep all encompasses your Brand.

As mentioned earlier, one of the worst sayings we have adopted in the body of Christ is, "I don't care what people think about me"! Really? Most everything we do in life is based on the upkeep of our image.

Regardless of how impressive your resume is; you get the job based on what the perception is of you by the interview committee during the interview process. Regardless of how good of a smooth talker you are, the person accepts your invitation for a date based on their perception of you at the time you two interact. No matter if you have all the fees to be processed into a fraternity or sorority, it is the perception they have of you during the intake process and how you carry yourself around campus that will determine if you are accepted. No matter how big the diamond on the engagement ring is, the woman accepts your proposal to marriage based on her perception of your ability to be a good husband (or, at least, we hope it is not based on the size of the diamond).

This even holds true biblically, our ability to effectively win souls to the Kingdom is partly based on our image or our "light." There are several scriptures that deal with Image and perception.

- Philippians 2:[15] *(ESV), "That you may be blameless and innocent, children of God without blemish in the midst of a crooked and twisted generation, among whom you shine as lights in the world,"*

- Acts 13:[47] (ASV)"*For so the Lord has commanded us, 'I have placed you as a light for the gentiles, that you may bring salvation to the end of the earth.'*"

- Romans 14:[16] (ASV) "*Therefore do not let what is for you a good thing, be spoken of as evil*".

- 1 Samuel 16:[7] (ESV), But the Lord said to Samuel, "*Do not look on his appearance or on the height of his stature, because I have rejected him. For the Lord sees not as man sees: man looks on the outward appearance, but the Lord looks on the heart.*" (man looks at appearance, but God looks at the image of your heart)

- 2 Corinthians 5:[17] (ESV) "*Therefore, if anyone is in Christ, he is a new creation. The old has passed away; behold, the new has come*". (there should be something different that people see)

So let's examine this for a moment. Let me ask you a question, Why did Jesus perform miracles? Did he do it to show how much power he had? Did he do it to mesmerize people and awe them with his wondrous works? No, he did it because he needed a Witness so that he could develop His Brand. That Brand Jesus wanted to develop here on Earth was the Kingdom of God. And the world understands the branding concept better than the church.

On May 21ˢᵗ, 2003 LeBron James, right after high school, signed a contract with Nike for seven years that was worth 90 million dollars. Nike gave him one word for his marketing campaign. That word was "Witness". Witness is a religious concept, and it comes from the Greek word, **martus** or **martur** (whence Eng., "martyr," *one who bears witness by his death*) OR "*one who can or does what he has seen or heard or knows*."

Nike was so bold to say that all you have to do is (WITNESS) LeBron James play basketball one time and based off what you have witnessed you will believe (BE CONVERTED) that he is the best basketball player in the world. After which, you will go on social media and be his (DISCIPLE) by following him on Twitter, Instagram, Facebook, YouTube, etc. . After you have chosen to follow him, you will then begin to (TESTIFY). How will you Testify? You will buy his shoes, jersey, tickets to his games, post comments about him on your personal Twitter, Facebook & Instagram pages? And by your testimony, you will be able to convert people to believe he is the best in the NBA as you were converted when you Witnessed him play, thus, building his BRAND.

LeBron James' promise is that he will be the best and do his best as a basketball player as you believe that he is the best. Nike made a marketing strategy off of Acts 22:¹⁵ "*For you will be a witness for him to everyone of what you have seen and heard*". Nike made LeBron the "him" and the fans the "witness".

So Levitical priests, what is your promise to your audience?

What do they see when they go to your Facebook page? What do they see when they go to your Instagram? What do they see when they pay $25.00 to come to your concert? Once they pay for your songs on iTunes, do you line up with what they purchased? Or is your response, "I don't care what folk think about me?" What if Jesus had said this during His three years of ministry? How many people do you think He would have won to the Kingdom?

We carry a mantle and if you are not using your gift, office, title or position to draw people to the Kingdom then your Brand is affected and infected. Your best ability to serve is to remember what do people Witness in you! As the Canon camera company marketing campaign slogan was in 1990, "Image is Everything".

"In a portrait, you have room to have a point of view,
the image may not be literally what's going on, but it's
representative"

Annie Leibovitz

PRAISE

"She (Leah) conceived again, and when she gave birth to a son she said, 'This time I will praise the Lord.' So she named him Judah. Then she stopped having children."

Genesis 29:35

Before we delve into Praise, we need to look at this passage of scripture. After Leah had given birth to Levi, hoping that Levi would finally cause Jacob to attach himself to her, she had one more child. And when she gave birth, she said, "this time I will praise the Lord." Then she stopped having children. Praise is significant in Service. Let's see why.

The significant thing to gather out of Genesis 29 is that you cannot always produce the desired results on your own by managing the situation. That regardless of your situation, you have to get to a point to where you are going to praise God and then, "stop having children". You are going to have to let go, "stop having children". Walk away from it, "stop having children". Quit trying to reason with it, "stop having children." End and excommunicate yourself from the situation, "stop having children". Take your hands off of it, "stop having children" and simply praise God in spite of it and let Him deal with it. Leah, after four children had to realize that this situation with her Jacob was something that she could not do on her own, so she got herself to a point where she was going to praise God and let it go.

This is significant because how many of us are leading praise and worship and compelling others to engage in it, and yet we have not "stopped having children?" We are bound by the very thing that we charge others to free themselves from. By "stop having children", what Leah did was take her attention off Jacob and put her attention on God. So let's look at what Praise really is.

What does Praise really mean?

The book of Psalms is a book of lyrical poems and prayers that are sung and is considered the "praise" book of the Bible, and it gives us thousands of reasons why praise is important, as well as examples of how to give praise to God. Primarily written by David, there is a Levitical presence as well from Heman, Asaph, and Ethan. One of my favorite scriptures concerning praise is Psalms 107:[8] *"Let them thank (praise) the LORD FOR HIS STEADFAST LOVE, for his wondrous works to the children of man!"*

SO IF JUDAH MEANS PRAISE…WHAT DOES PRAISE MEAN? IT MEANS:

- **EXPRESSIONS OF APPROVAL**

- APPRAISE, ASSESS, EVALUATE, MEASURE, VALUE

- THE STATE OF BEING APPROVED

- THE STATE OF BEING ADMIRED

- THE STATE OF BEING COMMENDED

When you do not praise God, what you are saying to Him is, I have not paid any attention to Your wondrous works. And what we don't understand is that you can't praise someone if you have not paid any attention to the things they have done. And when you do not praise God, He will get it from somewhere else that was not intended to give it in the first place.

In Luke 19:[40] *"He answered, 'I tell you, if these were silent, the very stones would cry out.'"*

The stones or rocks are inanimate objects, with no souls, spirit or emotion. They were not designed to praise (give attention to) God, but if those that are designed to praise God won't, then those things that were not intended to praise (give attention to) God... will. As Abraham Joshua Heschel so eloquently put it, *"Celebration is a confrontation, giving attention to the transcendent meaning of one's actions."*

When we reexamine Genesis 29, we will find that attention is one of the primary foundations of our Levitical meaning. Leah gave birth to a third son, Levi, hoping that this would cause Jacob to join/attach himself to her. Or in other words, cause Jacob to stop paying attention to Rachel and start pay attention to her by giving her his heart. Genesis 29:³⁴ *"Again she conceived and bore a son, and said, 'Now this time my husband will be attached to me, because I have borne him three sons.'" Therefore his name was called Levi.* For Jacob to "attach" himself to Leah, he had to stop praising or paying attention to Rachel.

Even in the natural, praise is important to the nature of man. It's a basic human need to have someone give us attention. We form relationships with those that have paid attention and accepted us.

But there is danger in not paying attention in the natural. We see the effects of it daily, but many times we do not understand the root of where those responses came from.

- WHEN YOU DON'T PAY ATTENTION TO YOUR DAUGHTER...a no good boy gets her attention.

- WHEN YOU DON'T PAY ATTENTION TO YOUR SON...a gang gets his attention.

- WHEN YOU DON'T PAY ATTENTION TO YOUR SPOUSE...an affair gets their attention.

- WHEN YOU DON'T PAY ATTENTION TO YOUR BOSS...the unemployment office gets your attention.

Not receiving praise or attention in your life for even minor things such as a new dress or tie, haircut or hairstyle, a report card or achievement of merit, causes the wall that would defend against those negative influences from coming in to be torn down.

141

In 2015, a tragedy took place in Charleston, South Carolina, where a gunman by the name of Dylan Roof walked into a historic African-American church and killed nine people. His uncle, Carson Cowles, noticed him in the police photo and turned him in however it was his interview to CNN concerning Dylan that was so telling about this young man. He stated that he told his sister, Dylan's mother, that he was too introverted. Cowles stated, *"I said this when he was like 19 years old, he still didn't have a job, a driver's license or anything like that and he just <u>stayed in his room</u> a lot of the time."* He was a loner, no one in his home paid any attention to this young man until it was too late.

So what is really being said when you don't pay attention…you are neglecting.

According to Vancouver Coastal Health, a world-class innovator in medical care, research and teaching, *"neglect is the **failure to provide necessary care, assistance, guidance or <u>attention</u>** that causes, or is reasonably likely to cause the person physical, mental or emotional harm or substantial damage to or loss of assets."*

Even at creation, the first thing that God saw that he did not like was <u>loneliness,</u> and He knew that man being alone would cause damage and harm. Genesis 2:[18] "The Lord God said, *'It is not good for the man to be alone. I will make a helper suitable for him.'*" God had already created the beasts of the land and the fowl of the air, but there was nothing suitable to be able to relate, procreate, and attend to the needs of the man. God realized that it was not good for the man to have no one around to pay any attention to him, thus woman was made.

In a further study, I found that loneliness is one of the reasons people leave the church, and it leads to divisions in the church. An article written by pathos.com explained:

"The feeling of being excluded, by definition, creates an intense loneliness. Being one of the only people living raw and authentically in a quest for community, is a lonely feeling. Being the one person who can't, in good conscience, sign onto the same statement of faith that the group has, is a lonely feeling. Watching cliques form as an outsider, and watching people who rise to esteemed positions by way of church politics, is a lonely feeling.

People leave church because they start to feel like an outsider, and that makes them lonely. It is an emotion that is painful, powerful, and given enough time, unbearable. If leaving church is what's needed to stop feeling so lonely and to stop feeling like an outsider— they'll do it. "

Sometimes it is not the lack of attention, but the attention given to the wrong things that produce an opposite effect on the church member or attendee. We give our attention to their attire, personality, or company they keep, and this has a negative effect on the church body as a whole.

According to a study by ChurchLeaders.com, *"...the way the formerly churched perceived the people within the church also motivated their leaving. Of the formerly churched who expressed dissatisfaction with those in the church, 45% said the other members were judgmental and hypocritical. In 1 Cor. 1:10, the Apostle Paul urged the church to preserve unity, having "no divisions" within the body."* Many times, the church member is driven to isolation and loneliness through judgment and condemnation by the "formerly churched".

According to a 2006 study conducted by Lifeway Christian Resources, *"The second most common category of reasons adults leave the church is "disenchantment with pastor/church," accounting for withdrawal of 37 percent of the formerly churched. The formerly churched say, church members "seemed hypocritical" (17 percent), "were judgmental of others" (17 percent) or "the church was run by a clique that discouraged involvement" (12 percent). These adults felt like outsiders looking in, revealing that the leadership and relational dynamics of a church can prove to be obstacles that prevent involvement. "While some may use disenchantment issues as a smokescreen to hide behind, the large percent of the formerly churched who struggle with disenchantment deserve some honest attention,"* Waggoner said.

Causing division in the Body of Christ leads to the members becoming lonely. In today's music ministry, we tend to cause great division within the divisions. There are cliques within choirs, praise teams, dance teams, intercessors, musicians, etc., that causes those that serve or desire to serve, to be pushed away.

Levitical Priests, do you only go into Praise when it is time to learn or teach the next new song to the praise team or choir? Do you only go into Praise when it is time for you to preach your next sermon? Do you only go into Praise when the dance ministry has been called to go forth in a special service or program? You have to ask yourself, does God hear from you when you are NOT on assignment. Do you spend too much time focusing on the non-essential aspects of the people that you lead that drives them to loneliness and isolation and eventually to a falling away from Christ? You need to ask yourself, do you spend any time paying attention, and not only to God but to the people you serve? If we are not praising, it limits our ability to serve. Have you noticed what God has done?

"I don't demand much. All I expect is for you to love me so much you kill yourself just to get my attention."

Jarod Kintz

WHAT'S IN YOUR EAR?

"Do not merely listen to the word, and so deceive yourselves.
Do what it says."

James 1:22

As we have learned, who you are listening too can be of detriment to you. In 2 Samuel 13, Amnon caused an issue in his family and subsequently got himself killed by listening to his advisor Jonadab, who put in his ear to rape his sister.

In Esther 1 King Xerxes listened to one of his advisors, Memukan, and divorced his wife because she would not put on her royal garments and crown and parade herself in front of his friends at a party. The Bible says in verse [16] *"Then Memukan replied in the presence of the king and the nobles, 'Queen Vashti has done wrong, not only against the king but also against all the nobles and the peoples of all the provinces of King Xerxes.* [17] *For the queen's conduct will become known to all the women, and so they will despise their husbands and say, 'King Xerxes commanded Queen Vashti to be brought before him, but she would not come.'* [18] *This very day the Persian and Median women of the nobility who have heard about the queen's conduct will respond to all the king's nobles in the same way. There will be no end of disrespect and discord.*

19 "Therefore, if it pleases the king, let him issue a royal decree and let it be written in the laws of Persia and Media, which cannot be repealed, that Vashti is never again to enter the presence of King Xerxes. Also let the king give her royal position to someone else who is better than she. 20 Then when the king's edict is proclaimed throughout all his vast realm, all the women will respect their husbands, from the least to the greatest.' 21 The king and his nobles were pleased with this advice, so the king did as Memukan proposed."

In chapter 2, "the Bible says that Later when King Xerxes' fury had subsided, he remembered Vashti and what she had done and what he had decreed about her." But before he could even consider revoking, one of his attendants pushed him to move toward seeking another woman to replace her which ended up being Esther.

I want to speak on not Who's in your ear, but What's in your ear. As a Levitical priest, not only must you watch the people that are speaking into you, but you have to watch the music that you are putting into you. Next to your eyes, the ears or sound has the most ability to influence behavior. In the Business Marketing world, this is called Sensory Branding, where marketing techniques are created that aim to seduce the consumer by using their senses to influence their feelings and behavior towards certain products. In the world of Medicine, scientists have found that music stimulates more parts of the brain than any other human function. Doctors use music as therapy and also are exploring how to use music as a way to heal people who have Parkinson's and Alzheimer's diseases.

Simply put, Music has power!

The greatest power of music is its ability to facility worship. What you constantly feed into your spirit is what you will eventually respond to. It will call unto you like a siren's song, forcing to you to answer. If music with sexual overtones is what you constantly feed into your spirit, then that is what you will find yourself doing. If music that speaks of disobedience to authority is what dominates what you put into your ears, then you will become rebellious. If music that speaks on experimentation is at the top of your music selection, then you will begin to try drugs and alcohol. If music with vulgar language is what you feed yourself, your tongue will become explicit. You cannot effectively be a worshipper when what you are constantly putting into your ears is not music glorifying, exalting and magnifying God. Your ear gate must be guarded at all times, not only with the words of people, but also from the music of the world.

"Music is the language of the spirit"

Khalil Gibran

COMMITMENT VS. TRUST

"Commit your way to the Lord; trust in him, and he will act."

Psalms 37:5

I recently watched the movie "Man of Steel". There was a segment where Kal-El or (Superman) is faced with a dilemma. General Zod and his military leaders have escaped from a celestial solitary confinement facility where, before they were sentenced, he vowed to hunt down Kal-El across the university for the DNA of the Kryptonian race that has been transferred to him by Kal-El's father. Superman is eventually located on Earth, and General Zod makes an ultimatum to him. *"Turn yourself over to us or we destroy Earth and all its inhabitants."* The young Superman, who is perplexed on what to do, wanders into a church and there he finds a preacher sweeping the floor. The preacher begins to have a discussion with him where Kal-El reveals to him that he is Superman and is the one that General Zod seeks. After a series of questions from the preacher, Superman decides that he can't trust General Zod, but is not sure if he can trust the humans either. As Superman gets ready to walk out the church, the preacher says to him, *"sometimes you have to take a leap of faith...the trust part comes later"*.

My daughter Mackenzie, when she was younger used to love to jump on the bed. She always wanted to play a game with me called Jump. She would tell me to move far back away from the bed, and she would go to the other end of the bed, run as fast as she could, then once she got to the edge, she would jump into my arms. Now Mackenzie never once concerned herself with trust before she jumped. She never questioned if I would catch her, she never was intimidated by the distance between her and me and the edge of the bed. Mackenzie just ran, got to the edge and committed herself to the jump first because the trust part came later...once she got in the air.

The enemy has tricked the Levitical priests and subsequently the Body of Christ into thinking that the problem with us is trust. The problem is not trust; it's commitment. We use trust as an excuse as to why we can't commit. We love to point fingers, we love to have a way out, we love to blame, and we love to have a trump card. But the order is to commit... which will cause God to act, then trust will manifest itself because it is the commitment that triggers God to act. This is confirmed in the scripture mentioned above Psalms 37:[5] *"Commit your way to the LORD; trust in him, and he will act."* God will act once we commit; then trust will initiate itself because we have committed (obedient).

There would be less marriage counseling among the Levitical priests if the couples quit blaming trust as the problem. Trust will manifest once you commit yourself to the marriage and to your assignment as husband and wife. The lack of trust is not the problem; it's a symptom.

There would be fewer issues among leadership if the leaders would commit themselves to the assignment first and not blame being overlooked in the past as the reason they can't trust. Trust will manifest once you commit yourself to the assignment.

The praise team would be more effective if the members committed themselves first. You being held back or overlooked in a past group, at a former ministry, by a former leader, is not the problem. Trust will initiate itself once you commit to the assignment set before you.

So ask yourself,

- If the issue is trust…then why do you keep showing up to rehearsal?

- If the issue is trust…then why do you keep attending the meetings?

- If the issue is trust…then why do you continue looking for an opportunity to teach/preach?

- If the issue is trust…then why won't you resign from your leadership position?

Levitical priests you must commit to your assignment…get to the edge…and take the leap. Whatever past hurts, issues, concerns or inhibitions will be overcome once you commit…then God will act…the trust part will come later.

"The best way to find out if you can trust somebody is to trust them."

Ernest Hemingway

WORK VS. WORSHIP

Don't let your work supersede your worship.

"A false balance is abomination to the Lord, but a just weight is his delight"

Proverbs 11:1

As you read the title, you may be thinking that I am speaking of how your worship (relationship) with God is. But that is not what this chapter is about. It's not at all about allowing your work as a musician, singer, dancer, preacher, intercessor, teacher, and other Levitical priesthood positions interfere with your worship to God. Let's look more closely…

In the scripture mentioned above, King Solomon is surveying the temple grounds and sees merchants who are selling goods to the people. But what he noticed is that the merchants are not honest businessmen. They are using unbalanced scales and giving the consumer fewer goods than what they paid for. Not only was he as King not happy with this, but this was also displeasing to God.

One of the many things Levitical priests focus on is Work, securing the next assignment. Once we achieve that, we spend all of our time trying to make that workplace where we minister better, so we take on more work to enhance the music ministry, or our paycheck becomes the driving force, so we take on more work to increase our income. For those that are single, this strategy may work depending on your family dynamic. But for those that are married, it can be detrimental. The enemy has attacked marriages among the Levitical priests because we forget about our first ministry, and that is to our spouse, and we forget or stop coming together in worship with them.

Every married couple should belong to the same church (covering), get the same Word (teaching), and attend at least one service a week together (worship) that is not dependent on if you are on schedule to Work. It's great if you can work and worship at the same place, but if you can't, you need to build a consistent time to come together. Just like you do to come together to rehearse to learn your music for your assignment or just as you come together with other preachers to get revelation for your message on Sunday.

The two biggest music mistakes I made as a musician in my marriage was taking work at two prominent churches in Chicago. Not because something was necessarily wrong with the respective pastors or their ministries, but because at that time, I needed to be with my wife. I should not have been at one particular church for 1 or 2 rehearsals during the week and three services on Sunday and not attending 1 with my wife regularly. I should not have been at the other church on Tuesday night Bible study (because that was pay night); I should have been at Bible study with my wife at our home church or spending more time ministering to her.

These churches were Work. And I found that I was spending more time at the Workplace than where I needed to be at home or at service (Worshiping) with my spouse. And what happens is we are not sober, which means, *"marked by temperance, moderation, or seriousness."* We don't moderate our work, and we lose our vigilance. Vigilance means, *"keeping careful watch for possible danger or difficulties."* We are so caught up in Work and saving the people that many times are not listening to us, that we are not paying attention to the enemy...and we fail to realize that he is paying attention to us.

1 Peter 5:[8]*"Be sober, be vigilant; because your adversary the devil, as a roaring lion, walketh about, seeking whom he may devour."* First, you must notice that the devil is called an adversary. This simply means that he is our enemy. He is not our friend, confidant, buddy or pal. He wants to take us down. Second, is that the devil is equated to *"a roaring lion"*. What we must remember is that the devil is a predator, not a scavenger. He doesn't attack dead meat; you can't kill something that isn't alive. Third, is that it says the devil *"walketh about seeking."* Satan is looking for an opportunity, going about the Earth. The servant Job was chosen by Satan to attack, Job 1:[6] *"Now there was a day when the sons of God came to present themselves before the Lord, and Satan came also among them. [7] And the Lord said unto Satan, 'Whence comest thou?' Then Satan answered the Lord, and said, 'From going to and fro in the earth, and from walking up and down in it."* Satan walketh about looking for opportunities, but before he can get an opportunity, he's got to SEE the opportunity first.

The enemy SEES you when you are attending services, concerts, events and speaking engagements alone, and your spouse is not with you. He SEES when you have your wedding ring on one week and have it off the next. He SEES when you are sitting in your car or standing in the hallway arguing on your cell phone with your spouse. He SEES what type of drink you like after you preach or if you prefer dark towels to white towels to wipe the perspiration off your face. He SEES what type of food you bring back to the church from lunch, so if you miss lunch, they know exactly what to bring you. He SEES you standing in the hallway or church parking lot talking to that man or woman when everyone knows you two are interested in one another. He SEES who responds to all your Facebook posts and likes all your pictures on Instagram. He SEES when you come to worship frustrated because you've been mad at your spouse all week. He SEES when something isn't right and moves cunningly, strategically.

I'm not saying you should not Work in music at a different ministry, take care of your family, push the Kingdom of God, that is part of your assignment as a married Levitical priest. But make sure that your Work does not cause your Worship to become eliminated...if so...you will find yourself infiltrated, separated, the marriage truncated, and the family devastated.

Musicians, preachers, prophets, intercessors, singers, dancers... do not spend all your time doing church work. Not only are you out of Order, but you are also out of Service. There are too many Levitical priests homes being broken up not because you are a bad person, but because you have become unbalanced in how you manage Work and Worship. Maintaining your marriage and family is a form of worship. If the music ministry has taken precedent over your home, whether intentionally or unintentionally, then you need to get back in alignment.

If home is not properly attended to, it hinders your ability to give service to God. You cannot make church work, whether paid or volunteer, more important than home, even if you have the support. The enemy will seek an opportunity and use the first chance he gets to sabotage anything in your marriage and/or family. Our homes are not attacked because we are so anointed; they are attacked because we are out of balance. And as Satan is walking about, he sees an opening and goes for the kill. So, make more time for dates and weekend get-a-ways, attend your daughter's softball games and your son's basketball game. Visit your parents, hang out with your siblings. Don't spend all of your time trying to save the world...and yours is coming unglued.

Remember, a just weight, "balanced life" is His delight; or what the ancients called, "a perfect stone." Because they used stones for weights; Not to give just weight, but also <u>for a just measure</u>, and to do justly in all civil dealings with men, is what God requires, and is well pleasing in his sight.

Work/Worship are not enemies. They should co-exist and be in harmony with one another. So if there is unbalance in your life, change the ".vs" to "and" and watch the scales become balanced again.

"There comes a time when you just have to say, "No!" – to the requests and to the system."

Fennel Hudson

SECURITY

"Through You we will push back our adversaries; Through Your name we will trample down those who rise up against us."

Psalm 44:5

Today, I was awakened by yet another scandal as the internet is all abuzz about someone among the Levitical priesthood who has been caught with a secret life. We are not immune to secrets. We all have them to one degree or another. Something that we hope never gets out from either our past or present that would change the opinions of how people think of us and possibly our ability to Witness. Maybe it's an addiction, a habit, an issue, a relationship, a lifestyle or a love child that we hope stays hidden from our family, boss, church, spouse or friends. But one thing we do know is that there is nothing going on now, that has not been going on before. However, what is more interesting is the frequency of such revelations. Is it due to technology and simply the invention of a cell phone with a camera? Is it God's grace period ending because we have not heeded to His warning signs or a combination of both? Is it the callousness of people who do not care about their own lives, let alone someone else's or just a vengeful person who can't seem to corral their emotions and wants to make others feel the pain they feel? We hear the traveling preacher and prophet go across the country preaching that this is the year of exposure. Or is it that the internet has made it easy for people to tell everything they know?

Whatever the case, I was talking to Debra "Snoopy" Hannah, an executive with a major record label, about an issue that became public about one the country's top gospel singers. And how this affects not only the church, but the gospel music industry as a business every time something like this comes out, and she said she always tells the artists she works with that, "You must protect your kingdom." When these things happen, it not only affects the ministry of the church, the pastor, and its members, but it also affects the artist's album sales and hinders the record label's ability to effectively market and promote.

Now you may be saying, well, there is only one kingdom and that is the kingdom of God, well you are wrong there. Satan has a kingdom also. He [Jesus] knew what they were thinking and said to them, "*Every kingdom divided against itself is laid waste, and no city or house divided against itself will stand. If Satan casts out Satan, he is divided against himself; how then will his kingdom stand?*" Mathew 12:25-26. The world's system is the kingdom of Satan, and that is any system that opposes the knowledge of God and the truth of the message of good news which is Jesus Christ.

When I began to look up the natural definition of Kingdom, it says that a kingdom is "*a country, state or territory ruled by a king or queen."* Among the synonyms that stood out to me was Domain and Province. We are establishing and advancing God's Kingdom but within that he has given us a Territory, Domain or Province that we are responsible for and in that, we are to protect it so that the Kingdom of God is not tarnished.

Your kingdom may be as a worship leader, choir director, pastor, musician, intercessor or it simply may be that your kingdom is your marriage. When we continually walk in sin, we can no longer effectively protect that territory, domain or province that God has given us to rule and we eventually become infiltrated and become exposed. Exposure causes damage to our ability to effectively witness and minister. Make sure that not only you have intercessors guarding the gates of the ministry, but have intercessors guarding you.

Avoid all pitfalls and use your way of escape. 1 Corinthians 10:[13] *"No temptation has overtaken you except what is common to mankind. And God is faithful; he will not let you be tempted beyond what you can bear. But when you are tempted, he will also provide a way out so that you can endure it."*

"You must protect your kingdom"

Debra "Snoopy" Hannah

GETTING GOD'S ATTENTION

"Do nothing from selfishness or empty conceit, but with humility of mind regard one another as more important than yourselves; do not merely look out for your own personal interests, but also for the interests of others. Have this attitude in yourselves which was also in Christ Jesus,"

Philippians 2:3-5

In this season, the music ministry that seeks to have a habitation from the Lord and not a visitation is going to gain it through two areas, Ministry and Worship.

In 2013, there was a song composed by the artist Pharrell, the song was called, "Happy." It became an international hit and the anthem to the World. People from every nation, language, creed and religion were singing this song. Pastors made the song part of their weekly sermons. Groups, Choirs, Praise Teams, and Youth Ministries made it part of their regular song list. As well as companies, associations, motivational speakers and even parents incorporated this song into their daily activities. But you want to know why this song has received such acclaim? Because it is a song of Ministry.

"Happy" has stopped people from committing suicide, brought folk out of depression, repaired marriages, turned pessimism into optimism, sparked someone to complete their degree, and even at the most minute level, it speaks LIFE into everyone's day who hears it.

In an interview with Oprah, Pharrell described how his whole intent behind the song was ministry. But even when he initially released the song, it never took off. Why? Because in ministry, God wants the credit and will get it even if the person or group behind the ministry is not saved or a Christian. This song became popular not because the name behind the song because if so, it would have made an initial splash when it was released, but it became popular only on the motives of ministry because Pharrell wrote the song for that purpose.

This same effect happened over 25 years ago in 1988 when a young man named Bobby McFerrin released a song called, "Don't Worry, Be Happy". This song reached #1 on the US pop charts and is the only song in history to reach this feat as a song sung A Cappella (without instruments). McFerrin recorded it using only his body to make all the sounds. During this time, there was no internet, smartphones, tablets, YouTube or social media, but the song became a worldwide sensation. Why? Because "Don't Worry, Be Happy" was a song of ministry.

Bobby McFerrin, in an interview with NPR, when asked how he felt about being a Pop star in the 80s replied, "*It wasn't about being famous or being a celebrity.*" Bobby saw a poster of an Indian guru named Meher Baba that had the four words "*Don't Worry, Be Happy*" on it and thought to himself that it was a pretty neat philosophy in 4 words. The song was able to minister because his motive behind it was not to write a song to become famous or rich.

Ministry is not tied to a denomination, race or nationality. It meets people exactly where they are. Many times the church has become guilty of saying that if Jesus were alive today, He would not be in the church, but in the world. Yet, what are the music ministries, gospel artists and the church doing that minister to people? I'm talking more than songs, concerts, and album releases, but the intent behind the songs, event and also our application of ministry in the church. Jeremiah 8:[22] "*Is there no balm in Gilead? Is there no physician there? Why then is there no healing for the wound of my people?*" That balm is Jesus, and the physicians are US, but yet, people seem not to be getting healed. Why? Because we that are responsible for carrying God's anointing have not yet been healed so there is no healing for the wounds of the people.

The smallest ministries in the church are in fact those that deal with ministry. Prisons, shelters, hospitals, clinics, sick and shut-in, prayer and deliverance, foreign missions, etc., are ministries that we can't get people to join. But anything that allows us to be "visible" requires a wait list. People are fighting to get into such ministries as the choir, praise team or to preach and be on the ministerial, prophetic and pastoral staff and once in, complain why they are not up front to direct, lead or speak.

An album release concert, anniversary concert, spring/summer concert generally is NOT ministry...it's promotions. YouTube clips, Facebook, Instagram, and websites are not ministry...it's marketing. Yes, it is a tool that must be done as an artist, church or entity to be successful and when used in a proper format, can be used to minister, but are we truly using it to promote God and not ourselves? What are we doing that promotes ministry and not marketing? What are we doing besides singing at church for Bible study and Sunday service? Is there a service/ministry component part of your schedule, itinerary, or plan?

The other area that must be accomplished to get God's attention is Worship. In 1 Samuel, God spoke to the judge Samuel and told him that I have found a man after my own heart. What does this mean in addition to conviction which was discussed earlier in chapters? This means that David worshiped God, but not only did he worship God, the intent/motives behind his worship was pure and not sparked because he wanted God to do something. David has God's heart...he attached himself to God. David secured God's attention when he was a nobody, when he was a shepherd boy, when he was alone, when he had no title or position, even when his family didn't remember him. God took a simple sheep herder and made him King due to his worship.

If your worship is sparked because you are paid to lead worship at your local church, then it is not worship. If your worship is ignited because you are in "concert mode", then it is not worship. If your worship is proposed because you are in the pulpit, then it is not worship. Where is your heart in the matter?

"The quickest way to get someone's attention is to no longer want it"

Knor

TIPS FOR SERVICE

- ## Rotate Assignments

  A music ministry can never be or get too big when there are assignments. Have personnel rotate services, so everyone gets an opportunity to serve at all service times and events scheduled in the temple. This helps keep entitlement at bay.

- ## Avoid Burnout

  If you have lost your desire and passion, your season might be up...transition. If you have lost your talent and anointing...its up. Don't let the public become aware of the latter before you do. Your downfall will not be ceremonious.

- ## Heart Check

  Make sure that you do not allow your flesh to take over to where you seek vain glory. You must keep your heart in the right place.

- ## Dedication

  Colossians 3:[23] *"Whatever you do, work at it with all your heart, as working for the Lord, not for human masters"*. Be committed, not because of pay, position or posture but because of service to the Lord. Make sure you do every task with equal dedication.

- <u>Know when to retire.</u>

There is never a time limit on being a servant, but this is a time limit on your service. Never stay too long, know when your time is up. The Retirement of the Levites; Numbers 8:[23] *"And the Lord spoke to Moses, saying,* [24] *"This applies to the Levites: from twenty-five years old and upward they shall come to do duty in the service of the tent of meeting.* [25] *And from the age of fifty years they shall withdraw from the duty of the service and serve no more.* 26 *They minister to their brothers in the tent of meeting by keeping guard, but they shall do no service. Thus shall you do to the Levites in assigning their duties."* (Under King David, he started training at age 20, not 25 years of age). This does not mean that at 50 you must stop because we all have started at various times, but there is an END date, and you need to know when that is. When you don't, you will begin to become stale and stink, and you will become a hindrance to the music ministry and no longer be an asset.

LEVITICAL CHARACTERISTICS

The Davidic Era

D avid was not a Levite, however, as previously mentioned, he was from the Tribe of Judah. He was our brother. And as we did with Moses, there are some characteristics that if you are a Levite, which you must also possess from your brother, Judah. The fourth child of Leah and Jacob.

Heart of God

I Samuel:13:[13] "Samuel said to Saul, '*You have done a foolish thing*,' Samuel said, '*You have not kept the command the* LORD *your God gave you; if you had, he would have established your kingdom over Israel for all time.* [14] *But now your kingdom will not endure; the* LORD *has sought out a* <u>*man after his own heart*</u> *and appointed him ruler of his people, because you have not kept the* LORD's *command.*'" What does this mean?

In 2013, I went to Washington, D.C. to visit my brother for three days. While there, I couldn't sleep. I was completely restless; I even slept in the chair sitting straight up for both nights that I was there. It was a struggle for me because I was contemplating this topic of David. The only man in the Bible to be mentioned as having the heart of God. But how could this be? I mean what did he do to gain this distinction that no one else seemed to be able to possess? And then on my flight back to Chicago, God explained it to me.

In 2012, one of the greatest movies of all-time was released, it was called, "The Avengers." At the time, this movie ranked 3rd on the all-time highest grossing movies worldwide at a staggering 1.5 billion dollars just behind "Avatar" and "Titanic". In this movie, there is a scene where Thor is locked up in a containment unit and Loki, Thor's brother, is about to dispose of his brother by dropping the containment unit to the ground. A S.H.I.E.L.D. agent named Phil Coulson has arrived, and he has a weapon that he plans to use to kill Loki. However, Loki changes positions and ends up behind him and stabs Agent Phil Coulson with his saber. As Agent Coulson lies dying on the ground, he says to Loki, *"You are going to lose… It's in your nature"*. Loki replies, *"Your heroes are scattered…your floating fortress is falling from the sky…where is my disadvantage?"* and just before Agent Coulson shoots his weapon and dies, he responds… *"Because you lack conviction"*.

David not only committed adultery and had a man killed, but he conspired to have the man killed. He was disobedient and took a census of the people willfully violating God's command not to do this in 2 Samuel 24, and he spilled much blood and was not allowed to see the completion of the temple, 1 Chronicles 28. However, in spite of all this, David was a man after God's own heart because he was a man of conviction. Not because he was perfect, not because he made no mistakes, not because he did everything right, but because David cared about the things that God cared about. What mattered to God, mattered to David. When David errored, he sought to correct it. When he ventured away from God, he sought to return.

Do you know who the most dangerous persons in the world are? Those that lack conviction. Those that can care less, those that don't know when enough is enough, those that don't think they can error, those that don't care who they hurt.

To be an effective Levitical priest, you MUST have conviction. Conviction won't keep you from error 100% of the time, but it will correct you 100% of the time because you will concern yourself with, how it affects God.

Skill and Anointing

1 Samuel 16:*14 "Now the Spirit of the LORD HAD DEPARTED FROM SAUL, AND AN EVIL SPIRIT FROM THE LORD TORMENTED HIM.*

15 Saul's attendants said to him, "See, an evil spirit from God is tormenting you. 16 Let our lord command his servants here to search for someone who can play the lyre. He will play when the evil spirit from God comes on you, and you will feel better."

17 So Saul said to his attendants, "Find someone who plays well and bring him to me."

18 One of the servants answered, "I have seen a son of Jesse of Bethlehem who knows how to play the lyre. He is a brave man and a warrior. He speaks well and is a fine-looking man. And the LORD IS WITH HIM."

23 Whenever the spirit from God came on Saul, David would take up his lyre and play. Then relief would come to Saul; he would feel better, and the evil spirit would leave him."

There is an argument in the church that all you need is the anointing. And there is another argument that if you are highly skilled, the anointing will be generated from your skill-set. Both arguments are wrong. Levitical Priests are supposed to be both skilled and anointed. Look in the passage of scripture where in verse 15 it says that attendants had found someone *"who can play"* some translations of the Bible use the word *"cunning."* This represents the natural part of David as a musician. He knew his instrument, knew chords and sounds and knew how to handle his instrument.

As we go down to verse 18, it states that *"The Lord is with him."* This represents the anointing. God's presence rested on David, and when he combined both the skill and anointing together, verse 23 took place, *"then relief would come to Saul; he would feel better, and the evil spirit would leave him"*.

It is important as Levitical Priest that we possess both skill and anointing if we are to be effective in our assignment.

PRAISER

1 Chronicles 29:*10* *"David praised the Lord in the presence of the whole assembly, saying, 'Praise be to you, Lord, the God of our father Israel, from everlasting to everlasting. 11 Yours, Lord, is the greatness and the power and the glory and the majesty and the splendor, for everything in heaven and earth is yours. Yours, Lord, is the kingdom; you are exalted as head over all. 12 Wealth and honor come from you; you are the ruler of all things. In your hands are strength and power to exalt and give strength to all. 13 Now, our God, we give you thanks, and praise your glorious name.'"* You should be seen praising. You can't praise

internally and in your mind, it is something that is demonstrated.

HE HAD A PLAN

As previously discussed, David had a plan for the temple and the Levitical priests, you can't have an effective music ministry without one.

MAN OF PRAYER

Psalms 5:[1] *"Listen to my words, Lord, consider my lament.*[2] *Hear my cry for help, my King and my God, for to you I pray.*[3] *In the morning, Lord, you hear my voice; in the morning I lay my requests before you and wait expectantly."*

Where is your relationship with God? We frequently want to demonstrate, but you find that many are not developing. We want to show off or demonstrate our beautiful girlfriend in public or post pictures of that new handsome man we have met on social media so that all can see and comment, but when you are not in public... when you are not on the internet, what are you doing to develop that relationship when no one is looking? It works the same way with God. You develop your relationship with God through prayer. Not by publicly praying when you are on duty at the Temple or when people are looking from the pews. But as Matthew 6:[5] *"And when you pray, do not be like the hypocrites, for they love to pray standing in the synagogues and on the street corners to be seen by others. Truly I tell you, they have received their reward in full.*[6] *But when you pray, go into your room, close the door and pray to your Father, who is unseen. Then your Father, who sees what is done in secret, will reward you."*

David was a man of prayer AS WELL AS praise. David's praise was simply an outward manifestation of what he did in private. So my question to you is what are you doing with God in private?

Not only pray for yourself, but also pray for others. Philippians 2:³"*Do nothing from selfishness or empty conceit, but with humility of mind regard one another as more important than yourselves;*"

John Calipari, Head Coach of Kentucky Basketball, was interviewed in 2015 by ESPN, and he stated that he goes to Mass every morning to pray. He said, "*I don't go to pray for myself. I never pray for myself…always for others. Life becomes easier when you put others first.*"

THE DOWNFALL OF THE LEVITICAL PRIEST

Strange Lovers & Intimate Conversations

During time of meditation in 2014, God shared with me that there will be two names that will be the downfall of the Levitical Priest and those names were, Solomon and Sampson.

Solomon

1 Kings 11:¹*"Now King Solomon loved many foreign women, along with the daughter of Pharaoh: Moabite, Ammonite, Edomite, Sidonian, and Hittite women, ² from the nations concerning which the LORD HAD SAID TO THE PEOPLE OF ISRAEL, 'YOU SHALL NOT ENTER INTO MARRIAGE WITH THEM, NEITHER SHALL THEY WITH YOU, FOR SURELY THEY WILL TURN AWAY YOUR HEART AFTER THEIR GODS.' SOLOMON CLUNG TO THESE IN LOVE."*

As we examine this, the Bible gives two distinct reasons for Solomon's downfall. One, he had many lovers and two, he also had foreign or what some translations say, strange lovers. And these many lovers turned his heart away from God to their Gods. Why? Because Solomon held on to them and desired them in love.

In this season, our downfall will be due to our continued

relations with many strange/foreign lovers. But in this time, it is not limited to sexual sins and relationships with the opposite sex as it was for Solomon. In this season, the strange lover will be pornography, gambling, alcohol, marijuana, discord and various other inhibitions and your attachment or (clinging to these in love) will cause your heart to be turned away from God and cause you to be exposed. When you fall under the power of attraction and cling to these lovers, your heart will seek fulfillment from them, and your desire for God will wane.

And what will happen once your heart is turned away? When you minister, it will be like BABEL upon the ears of the people. That strange lover will always be present with you. It will accompany you, and it will stand before you. Your songs, your words, your choreography, your leadership and your sound will fall upon the ears and sight of people and take no effect, and they will not be able to even comprehend you. It will be as if you are singing and speaking in a foreign language. You won't be received; breakthrough and deliverance will not take place because the anointing has fled from you. People will not see God...but the many and strange lover(s) that are present which accompanies you.

In this time, the Levitical Priest must divorce themselves and seek deliverance from the strange lovers that have attached themselves to us. If you do not, then 1 Kings 11:⁹, *"And the Lord was angry with Solomon, because his heart had turned away from the Lord, the God of Israel, who had appeared to him twice ¹⁰ and had commanded him concerning this thing, that he should not go after other gods. But he did not keep what the Lord commanded. ¹¹ Therefore the Lord said to Solomon, "Since this has been your practice and you have not kept my covenant and my statutes that I have commanded you, I will surely tear the kingdom from you and will give it to your servant."* Will happen.

For many of us, God has spoken to us, twice or several times, he has given us grace and a way of escape and if no change takes place, your kingdom, domain or territory which God has given you He will tear from you and give it to someone else.

Sampson

Judges 16:[5] *"And the lords of the Philistines came up to her (Delilah) and said to her, 'Seduce him, and find out where his great strength lies..."*

Judges 16:[15] *"And she said to him, "How can you say, 'I love you,' when your heart is not with me? You have mocked me these three times, and you have not told me where your great strength lies." [16] And when she pressed him hard with her words day after day, and urged him, his soul was vexed to death. [17] And he told her all his heart, and said to her, "A razor has never come upon my head, for I have been a Nazirite to God from my mother's womb. If my head is shaved, then my strength will leave me, and I shall become weak and be like any other man."*

Many think that Sampson's downfall was due to him lying with Delilah, it was not if you read the book of Judges, Delilah was not the first woman he had been with; Delilah was just the woman he got caught up with. Sampson's downfall was not due to sex, but due to what he shared.

Some people want to get close to you because there are things they want to know, and they are being sent by others who know you can be enticed. In verse 5, the Philistines sent a woman to get close to Sampson. The Philistines knew that Sampson had a taste for women and promiscuity because he had previously gone to Gaza to see a harlot. Remember, the enemy will send your weakness to you because they have become aware of it.

Notice in the scripture in verse 16 where it says, "*...she pressed him hard with her words day after day, and urged him, his soul was vexed to death.*" Vexed in Greek is a word that means "Qatsar" which means to "wear down." Delilah questioned and bugged Sampson about the source of his power to the point where she wore him down, and he ended up sharing something with her that he should not have. Sampson had an intimate conversation with Delilah. Be cautious of people who constantly question, prod and pry about the intimate and personal things of you. Their intentions are to destroy you with the information they gather.

Today's Levitical Priest is involved in far too many intimate conversations with people, sharing personal, private and sacred information and technology has made this easier for us to do so. Smartphones, tablets, the internet and social media...we are spending more time talking with people that we don't know and should not be talking too, than we do with people that we know, such as our spouses, children, parents, and spiritual support.

And as music industry leaders, in our effort to be more "marketable", we have formed superficial relationships with people and we are too transparent. The enemy then goes back in sabotage and lays an ambush for us for what we have shared with them. In turn, we lose our effectiveness to minister because we have shared too much. We have shared the source of things. Our struggles, our pain, our weaknesses & temptations, our passions, areas where we need deliverance; we've discussed our marriage and relationship;

our anointing to people that seek to exploit us.

In this time, the Levitical Priests must guard themselves against strange lovers and intimate conversations. Once people find out about your strange lover(s) through intimate conversations, adversaries will rise up against you, and they will begin to speak publicly of it to persecute you and eventually sabotage the ministry, and you will soon be brought down. Testify…but make sure you have overcome.

"Do not become a victim to your own transparency"

Michael Weatherspoon

TIPS FOR MUSIC MINISTRIES THAT ARE ARTISTS

- Your first assignment is the Flock...not your Fans.

Church music ministries that are artists have a hard time navigating this area. You have to make sure the church is covered, but you must do engagements to promote the album. Over and over you find that the church that does a recording only has one music entity that serves the entire church. They are the only choir or praise team and that church usually has only 1 set of musicians to cover all services. That in and of itself creates problems for coverage at the church and limits their ability to meet the demands of the consumer. The Pastor, Minister of Music and record label struggle and, at times, are at odds over how to meet all the spiritual and business demands.

So what tends to happen? The artistry takes precedent over the ministry. Simply put, when money and fame get involved if you are not careful, the assignment of covering the temple over the long-term takes a back seat to the short-term assignment of being an artist. So what can you do:

- Set rules of engagement at the point of auditions

Let potential ministry members know that the assignment for the ministry is to cover the temple. They are auditioning for the temple assignment. Anything on the artist side is not guaranteed nor promised. Letting the candidates know this up front will allow you to gauge their intent and weed out potential problems and makes sure that covering the temple stays as the primary responsibility.

- Make sure talent is consistent

  Let's not get deep here. 1 Samuel says that David was skilled and anointed. Talent plays a major part in your ability to be effective. But it also plays a part in the chemistry of the ministry. When you have a set of singers, musicians, dancers, speakers, etc., that are fundamentally better than the others, and you only take those out to represent the artist side of the ministry, you set up internal barriers among those that are members of that ministry. Remember, ALL should be talented enough to represent the ministry as artists, but ALL will not be used to represent the ministry as an artist because the first assignment is the temple.

- Set up temple assignments to keep the focus on the ministry and not the artistry.

  Typically, ministry leaders only set up personnel for service, which is Bible study and Sunday service(s). When you only do this, you create an environment where people only compete for what I call, "pulpit time." Ministry then equates to, "when am I scheduled to minister at service?" Assignments should be scheduled for: homegoing services, prayer watch/nights, weddings, ministerial and pastoral speaking engagements, outreach, etc. and this should be on a rotational basis.

Scheduling the music ministry to minister at other events besides the normal church times will keep an environment of service and ministry in the forefront.

- ## Keep personnel consistent

Rehearse together, but keep the scheduling of personnel consistent. I strongly suggest having a set "road team" and also having an A and B team to cover the temple. You should set a road team to represent the artist side. Why? As part of your artistry, as we discussed in the Service Chapter, your image is important. (Keeping a consistent look and team, aides you in your presentation, marketability, and ministry as an artist). Also, traveling and being on the road is an entirely different beast altogether. It brings its own set of problems and having a consistent team can aid in bringing resolution to issues quickly due to familiarity.

In having an A and B team, (which you can name them however you want, some are named Alpha and Omega teams), these teams develop "ministry chemistry" together. Vocal blends, dance movement, stage presence, chord progressions are developed when a team ministers consistently together. Do not set up scheduling where personnel changes from service to service. Does a coach change his starting line-up from game to game? NO. Neither should we in the church.

- ## Communicate! Communicate! Communicate!

Do not make the road team the elite team. Share all pertinent information to the home team so that the road team does not appear superior. Communication wards off tension. I've found that there are a lot of issues within music ministries because there is no honest and consistent communication. Too many secrets and unanswerable questions lead to mutiny.

- <u>Stay focused</u>

Keep the mission on service. No one is exempt from it. Everyone must still have an assignment in the temple and for ministry.

- <u>Manage your comments</u>

Make sure that public comments on the music ministry are more about ministry work and less about the successes as an artist. If the comments from the pulpit and on social media are constantly about record sales, radio play, tours, engagements, awards, etc. What this conveys to the membership and the music ministry is that money is being made, and I want to be part of it OR where is my money? One of the biggest arguments among church ministries that are artists is about money and opportunities to make it. And this is disguised under the umbrella of "ministry". If public comments remain ministry oriented, you will have less negative responses from the music ministry members. People respond to what they hear.

- <u>Know when the "artist" season is over</u>

Don't get to a point to where everyone knows your season is up but you. Ministry is always relevant, but the artistry is seasonal. Many music ministries struggle to become artists or hold onto past success, and you lose sight of what the real purpose was from the beginning. God allows us to be artists, but ministry is our assignment.

TIPS TO BE A SUC-CESSFUL MUSIC MINISTRY

- <u>Develop Chemistry</u>

I do not believe the church today truly understands how much being in a relationship with one another assists in your ability to minister more effectively. Do you talk during the week, visit one another, go out for pizza after rehearsal, go bowling or to the movies or out to dinner? Engaging in these things help develop chemistry which translates to better teamwork.

One of the things my brother, Daniel Weatherspoon, and I do before we record any artist in the studio or live is we spend a few months away from music just getting to know them. We hang out, invite them over to watch the basketball or football game, we go to dinner or go and visit their family. Why? Because we have learned that if we have a relationship away from the studio, it will translate into the interpretation of the music in the studio. It is the same in the Temple. The choir, praise team, dancers, gatekeepers should all have some type of relationship with one another.

Remember Relationships are more valuable than money!

- <u>Keep Perspective</u>

Church hurt is real; we do wrong to each other, and it causes scars, however, one of the other reasons people are in or leave the church hurting is because they have lost perspective. You must remember that the music ministry does not belong to you. You do not own it, don't act like you do. When you start taking ownership of things that you do not own, you have lost perspective, and you are heading for an emotional train wreck. You are a servant; you are not the owner. Remember, the pastor is allowing you to do the job, you are not the pastor, and you can be replaced at any time.

Leave the work of the Temple at the Temple. When you are with your family, spend time with your family. The order is 1. God, 2. Family, 3. Church. Church includes "church work". Leave church work at church. Do not let the work of church become more important that your marriage and family or you will soon lose your marriage and family.

- Invest in your Gift

You can always improve, learn and enhance your gift and skill set. Don't ever assume that you can't get better or be better. There is always something to learn. Not investing in your gift only brings your replacement that much closer to you.

- Keep your name clean

One of the worst things you can do to hinder your ability to serve is always having your name in mess and foolishness. Keep clear of things that can distract you, causing you to lose focus and get you in trouble. Remember, Scandal is fun to watch, but it isn't funny when you are the Scandal.

- <u>Music is an Art...not a Science</u>

How God wants to move today with this set of songs, may not be how He wants to move with the same set of songs tomorrow. Be open and an empty vessel to allow God to move in the music ministry as He sees fit and do not try and <u>calculate</u> what will happen.

- <u>Give</u>

Pay your tithes and offerings.

Pour back into someone. There can be no legacy without impartation.

MARCHING ORDER OF THE TRIBES OF ISRAEL
AS THEY TRAVELED EAST TO THE PROMISE LAND OF CANAAN:
Numbers 10:11-28

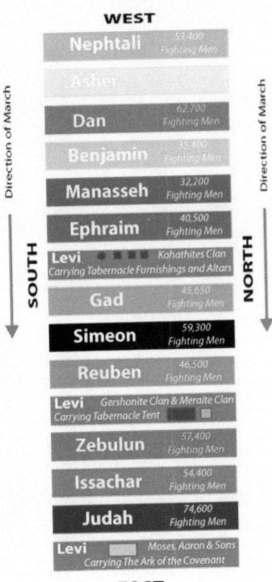

WEST

Nephtali — 53,400 Fighting Men

Asher

Dan — 62,700 Fighting Men

Benjamin — 35,400 Fighting Men

Manasseh — 32,200 Fighting Men

Ephraim — 40,500 Fighting Men

Levi — Kohathites Clan — Carrying Tabernacle Furnishings and Altars

Gad — 45,650 Fighting Men

Simeon — 59,300 Fighting Men

Reuben — 46,500 Fighting Men

Levi — Gershonite Clan & Meraite Clan — Carrying Tabernacle Tent

Zebulun — 57,400 Fighting Men

Issachar — 54,400 Fighting Men

Judah — 74,600 Fighting Men

Levi — Moses, Aaron & Sons — Carrying The Ark of the Covenant

SOUTH — Direction of March
NORTH — Direction of March

EAST

Music Ministry Flow Chart

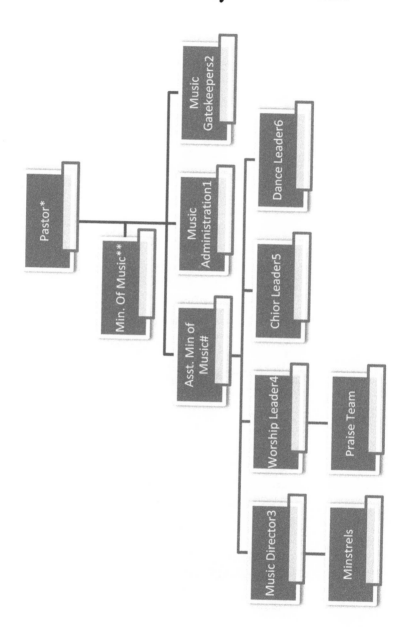

*The Pastor is the Chief Worship Leader. The worship in the temple cannot go any further than where the Pastor is personally in their worship.

**The Minister of Music is the Primary Worship Leader. They have been assigned to administrate the worship of the house by the Pastor. In the event that there is no Min. of Music, the Pastor is by default.

#The Assistant Minister of Music, reports directly to the Minister of Music and duties are assigned per their direction.

1. Manages administrative and fiscal needs for the music ministry to make sure thing flow efficiently.

2. The Gatekeepers are responsible for Spiritual Support. Assign Intercessors and Armor bearers to each music ministry and any spiritual edification should come from this area.

3. The Music Director is responsible for rehearsing and leading the minstrels.

4. Worship leader is responsible for the praise team. If there's more than one praise team, each team should have a worship leader to teach and instruct.

5. Choir Leader is responsible for the choir. If there's more than one choir, each choir should have a leader/director to teach and instruct.

6. Mime, Standards, Encouragers, Spoken Word and Sign Language should fall under the Dance Leader. (Sign Language should have its own space. Sign Language requires specific specialization). Each entity should have a leader/director to teach and instruct.

HOW DOES THIS LOOK IN TABERNACLE FORM

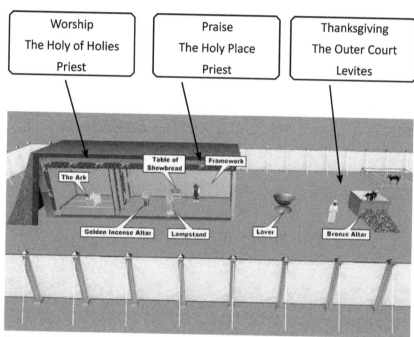

Worship	Praise	Thanksgiving
The Holy of Holies	The Holy Place	The Outer Court
Priest	Priest	Levites

Brazen Altar — Where we deal with our sin and overcome guilt.

Brazen Laver — Where we lay aside troubles, cares and fears, cleanse.

Table of Showbread — Where we submit our will to God and His Plan.

Golden Candlestick (lamp) — Where we win the battle of the mind.

Golden Altar of Incense — Where we release our emotions.

HOW DOES THIS LOOK IN HUMAN FORM

The temple and spirit of man

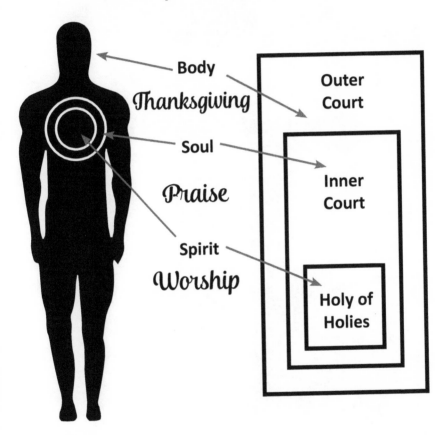

HOW DOES THIS LOOK IN TEMPLE FORM

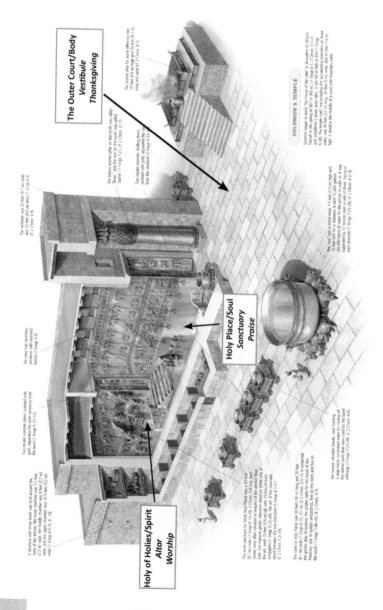

ABOUT THE AUTHOR

Michael Weatherspoon has been in the music industry for 30 years as a drummer, producer, consultant and label executive. Forming Spoonfed Productions with his brother Daniel Weatherspoon 20 years ago, has produced dozens of records for various gospel and inspirational artists under this banner around the world. Having performing on over 100 albums and DVDs as drummer during his career, Michael has gained valuable knowledge, insight and experience to help new and seasoned artists achieve their goals in their career. (to see Michael's full discography, go to: www. ___weatherspoon.com/discography/)

Chicago suburb of Harvey, Illinois and from South Suburban College and BA in ___ern Illinois University worked for 14 years ___n areas of admissions, assessment, cultural ___and retention and presented on these topics ___iversities and conferences around the country. ___, Michael was a contributing author for the ___s Springfield on the book, African American ___ Through Higher Education and Society.

___ugh 2011, Michael served as Team Leader for ___s Ministry at Valley Kingdom Ministries

What We Can Do For You

Instructional Videos, Video eBooks, Financing/Informatics, Real Estate Informatics, Business Plan Development and Informatics, Websites, Marketing Informatics, Commercials, Music Lessons Real Time/Online, Instructional/Historical Videos, Music Tracks, Medical Informatics, Music Transcription. Music performance: Single Man Acts to Big Bands

If a picture says a thousand words, how much Instructional INFORMATION can be put on display with a series of pictures/words presented in a video with music?

Post Office Box 14615, Houston TX 77221

International in South Holland, Illinois and through this developed a Levitical training series for new and current music ministry members. Since then, Michael has spoken to several church music and leadership departments, gospel artists and various leadership and music conferences on the importance of Levitical order. (to see all a list of Michael's events, go to: www. michaelweatherspoon.com/speaker/)

More From Faith Walk Publishing

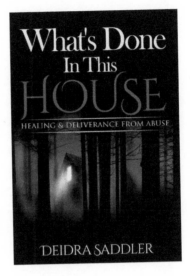

CPSIA information can be obtained
at www.ICGtesting.com
Printed in the USA
FSHW010154160419
57276FS